HELPING STUDENTS LEARN IN A

LEARNER-CENTERED ENVIRONMENT

HELPING STUDENTS LEARN IN A LEARNER-CENTERED ENVIRONMENT

A Guide to Facilitating Learning in Higher Education

Terry Doyle

Foreword by John Tagg

STERLING, VIRGINIA

Sty/us

COPYRIGHT © 2008 BY STYLUS PUBLISHING, LLC.

Published by Stylus Publishing, LLC
22883 Quicksilver Drive
Sterling, Virginia 20166–2102

Library of Congress Cataloging-in-Publication Data
Doyle, Terry, 1951–
    Helping students learn in a learner-centered environment: a guide to facilitating learning in higher education / Terry Doyle.—1st ed.
        p.   cm.
    Includes bibliographical references and index.
    ISBN 978-1-57922-221-5 (cloth : alk. paper)—
    ISBN 978-1-57922-222-2 (pbk. : alk. paper)
    1. College teaching.   2. Student-centered learning.   I. Title.
LB2331.D66   2008
378.1'7—dc22   2007038267

13-digit ISBN: 978-1-57922-221-5 (cloth)
13-digit ISBN: 978-1-57922-222-2 (paper)

Printed in the United States of America

All first editions printed on acid free paper
that meets the American National Standards Institute
Z39-48 Standard.

Bulk Purchases

Quantity discounts are available for
use in workshops and for staff
development.
Call 1-800-232-0223

First Edition, 2008

10   9   8   7   6   5   4   3   2   1

For Julie,
the love of my life

CONTENTS

FOREWORD

In this book, Terry Doyle addresses the central paradox that frustrates efforts to improve the quality of undergraduate education. For a variety of reasons, most of them good, college and university faculty these days are more interested in the learning processes of their students than ever before. Many faculty members and administrators are grappling with how to get their students to learn more and better. Yet in talking with educators about making our institutions more learning centered, the question I hear most often is "But how can we get the students on board?" At the root of the quest for more learner-centered institutions lies this paradox: Students, the learners, aren't convinced. Students need to be persuaded that learning is the central purpose of their schooling. They do not come to us believing this. And they are not necessarily comfortable with the idea of taking charge of their own learning. Indeed, much of the resistance—or apparent resistance—of faculty to new ways of teaching is rooted in the apparent intractability of students. How do you recognize the authority of students as learners, give students responsibility for their own learning when, essentially, they won't take "yes" for an answer?

Terry embarks from the realization that if we want to improve the quality of undergraduate education, we need to start where we are, not where we wish we were, or where we think we ought to be. And he correctly identifies the biggest challenge in taking a learner-centered approach: getting the learners to buy into it. Drawing on long experience as a classroom teacher as well as his work with teachers in many disciplines as a faculty developer, Terry is really addressing two audiences in this book The primary audience is, of course, college and university faculty. But the ultimate and long-term audience consists of the students in our classes, the learners who are the real decision-makers in this process. Consistently, throughout every chapter, he keeps this double focus. There is never any doubt that this book is mainly about students, and that its core message is to be offered to and shared with students.

This is not a book about teacherly sleight of hand, legerdemain, or clever techniques and moves that will allow us to trick students into remembering the stuff we want them to remember. Terry's message is utterly transparent. He is urging us not only to take a brain-based approach to teaching, but to show our students how their brains and memories work so that they can understand how to learn most effectively. He grapples with the hardest challenges that classroom teachers face when they try to give students responsibility for their own learning: getting them to work in groups, to give and take serious feedback on their work, to stand up and talk in front of a class, to take a deep approach so that their learning will last a lifetime, rather than a surface approach that produces learning that will fade at the end of the term. And in each case, he is talking to us about how to talk to students, how to shape students' tasks and roles, and how to engage students in designing their own learning environments. If the learning is going to get done, it is the students who are going to do it. Terry is consistently clear about this, and it shapes his approach in every chapter.

The apparent variety and complexity of the research on learning prevents many teachers from taking a more learner-centered approach in their own classrooms. The research on the brain and on cognitive processes points out new directions for teaching, but it seems to the casual observer to point out quite a few different new directions. Too many to keep track of all at once. And that research is often embedded in large books that look like major investments of time and attention. Even if the average professor of math or sociology did have time to keep current with research on the brain and cognitive science, the prospect of presenting it to her students—while still teaching math or sociology—would be daunting, to say the least. Terry has been keeping up on the research. And he has done a splendid service here by presenting the most important implications of research on learning concisely, accurately, and accessibly. In doing so, he not only explains it to us, but he helps us to see how we can explain these principles to our students. Even more importantly, he illustrates how we can shape our students' experience in the classroom so that they can discover many of these essential principles for themselves. The author has a clear bias, but it is a bias that emerges from the research: he consistently prefers to let students discover for themselves their own capacity as learners. Because, as he shows us over and over again, if they learn it for themselves, they really learn it.

Ultimately, I think that the paradox that our students pose for us is easily understood. Most of our students shy away from taking responsibility for their own learning because they think it will make things harder for them. They think it will be more work, with no clear reward. And, frankly, I think some of our faculty colleagues are a bit hesitant for the same reason. But they are wrong. What this book illustrates is that a deep approach to learning, and to teaching, can be richer without being harder and offer rewards that are not even accessible through surface approaches. Once they begin to see the long-term rewards, students and faculty will become engaged and committed to the learner-centered classroom.

For the individual teacher, this book offers a dozen points of entry to a more learner-centered approach to teaching. And it provides the apparatus for engaging students in the enterprise. But the greatest challenge of learner-centered teaching remains bringing the learners along. How much easier this would be, and how much more productive, if the approach that Terry describes here became the new standard, if it became the rule rather than the exception. Students resist taking responsibility for their learning because they aren't used to doing so. It is, for a depressingly large number of students, a new concept. But if many teachers at an institution adopted these principles, if a critical mass of teachers in a department or a faculty pursued learner-centered teaching as a goal, then it would multiply the benefits by orders of magnitude. If students came to see learner-centered teaching as normal, as the expected, as what most teachers do, teaching well would be vastly easier, and we would be much closer to fulfilling the promise of lifelong learning for all of our students.

John Tagg
Associate Professor of English
Palomar College
San Marcos, California

ACKNOWLEDGMENTS

To a great extent this book was 30 years in the making. The ideas in this book are the result of thousands of conversations about teaching and learning that I had with my many colleagues here at Ferris State, and I thank them all for their openness and willingness to share their ideas about teaching and learning. I have had more conversations with my lovely wife Julie than anyone else. For the past 23 years, Julie has taught in the Hospitality Programs here at Ferris State. We have spent many pleasurable hours discussing students, curriculum, and pedagogy, trying to develop ways to optimize our students' learning. I also want to thank my two children, Jessica, who served as my much-needed unofficial editor, and Brendan, who allowed me to use some of his personal school adventures in this book.

I am indebted to my close friends and colleagues, Mike Cairns and Dan Burcham, who, for the past 30 years, have been both sounding boards for my ideas and resources for increasing my understanding of how students learn. These men have greatly enhanced my work on teaching and learning. Thanks, too, to the many faculty members who participated in the workshops I facilitated on learner-centered teaching for their questions and insightful ideas about optimizing students' learning. Their contributions helped formulate the ideas for this book, especially those of Cecil Queen, Dan Adsmond, and Jennifer Johnson.

I especially want to thank Maude Bigford and Judith Hooper for their editorial help and their many years of friendship. I owe thanks, as well, to the nursing faculty at Ferris State for reading early drafts of chapters and providing very helpful feedback. Thank you also to Jennifer Cox for her many hours of help with the bibliography for this book and to Jessica Pawloski, who helped with many of the charts and drawings in the book.

The content in this book was enhanced by the work of Andrew Roberts of Middlesex University, who allowed me to use his examples of effective report and paper writing, and Professor Edward Vockell of Purdue University at Calumet, who allowed me to include his excellent examples of how to help students develop metacognition skills from his book, *Educational Psy-chology*. I also want to thank Maryellen Weimer, whose presentation on our campus 5 years ago set in motion my thinking about learner-centered teaching and led to many of the ideas in this book, and John Tagg, for his willingness to write the foreword to this book. Thanks, as well, to Milt Cox and Laurie Richlin, who welcomed me into the Lilly conference family 10 years ago and have given me outlets for my ideas on learner-centered teaching at the Lilly conferences. Finally, I want to thank Henryk Marcinkiewicz for helping me get started in faculty development work and for encouraging me to do more writing.

INTRODUCTION

I am one of those education lifers. Every fall since I was 5 years old, I have headed off to school, and I've been on one side of the desk or the other for the past 51 years. In that time I have experienced some amazing teachers, including Mr. Zelinski in 8th grade, and Sr. Marybride Ryan and Dr. Dave Yarington at Aquinas College. I have also experienced some of the poorest teaching ever perpetrated on a student. I learned in spite of some teachers and because of others. What I have learned from going to school for the past 51 years is that teachers can make learning fun, interesting, exciting, and challenging, or they can make it awful, boring, painful, and useless. Teachers can encourage learners or discourage them. My best teachers were not only encouraging and supportive, but they also taught me how to learn. They helped me not only to see the value of the content, but to grasp the greater value of being able to learn whatever I became interested in on my own.

Creating a learner-centered environment is the most important thing an educator can do to optimize students' learning. At first this concept might be a bit uncomfortable for students, most of whom are accustomed to teacher-centered learning experiences. Their learning has largely been controlled by teachers and, as students, they have had few, if any, choices about what and how to learn. They have spent most of their time in traditional learning environments, and, for most, their academic success has reinforced the value of those traditional experiences. Students have no reason to think their college learning experiences will be any different. As college- and university-level educators, we can, and should, change this.

A learner-centered environment *is* different. It requires students to take on new learning roles and responsibilities that go far beyond taking notes and passing tests. It is an environment that allows students to take some real control over their educational experience and encourages them to make important choices about what and how they will learn. In learner-centered classrooms, collaboration is the norm, not an occasional class activity.

These changes will initially be difficult for many students. Most will be uncomfortable with their new roles and responsibilities, and some will be downright hostile toward them. It is up to us, their teachers, to help them understand these changes and teach them how to learn in this new environment. We must work with them to develop the skills and knowledge they need to be successful in learner-centered classrooms. Our students are not prepared to do this on their own; it is too unfamiliar and requires too many new skills that many students do not possess. This book will guide you as you help your students adapt to learner-centered classrooms, teaching them new skills and making them comfortable with their new responsibilities.

Most important, students will need a clear understanding of why teaching has shifted from teacher-centered to learner-centered. They need to understand that teaching, like all professions, must allow research to inform its practice. They need to see that we are obligated to make changes in how we teach if research shows that those changes will improve our students' opportunities to learn. Bransford, Brown, and Cocking (2000), in their book, *How People Learn*, state it powerfully:

> Many people who had difficulty in school might have prospered if the new ideas about effective instructional practices had been available. Furthermore, given new instructional practices, even those who did well in traditional educational environments might have developed skills, knowledge and attitudes that would have significantly enhanced their achievements.

Our students will benefit from understanding the research that has motivated us to change our teaching practices, because this same research explains how they can become better learners. For example, most teachers who practice learner-centered teaching give cumulative exams, not to make their students' lives miserable, but because research on memory formation strongly indicates that cumulative exams, as opposed to exams for which students can cram, offer a greater opportunity for students to relearn repeatedly the most important information in the course, leading to a deeper understanding of material and long-term memory formations.

Three separate but related events have informed the writing of this book. The first was realizing, 5 years ago when I first started working with faculty on how to develop a learner-centered practice, that I had missed a very important step in their preparation. I had not discussed with them how they should prepare their students for the new roles and responsibilities they would be asked to take on in this new learning paradigm. I had been too "teacher-centered," and I'd forgotten about the learners. Old habits die hard. I realized that students would need a clear rationale for this change and a new set of skills that would enable them to be productive learners in learner-centered classrooms. I immediately began to develop strategies that would help my colleagues introduce learner-centered teaching to their students, and that would enable them to teach their students how to learn in a learner-centered environment.

The second event took place at the 2005 Professional and Organizational Development Network in Higher Education (POD) conference. As I looked at the session topics, I realized that many of them focused on how to teach, even those that dealt with learner-centered practice. I did not attend all of these sessions, so I don't know if the presenters addressed ways to help students learn, but the session titles reinforced the need to emphasize the students' role in learner-centered environments. I had already been thinking about that idea a great deal before the conference. In fact, the title of my session was "Helping Students Learn in a Learner-Centered Environment."

The third event was Stylus asking me to write this book. Publishers make it their business to know the needs and desires of the markets they serve. If learner-centered education was something on Stylus's radar, it confirmed for me that this topic should be addressed more formally. I already knew that if learner-centered practice was to be successful, then students would need clear reasons why they should adopt this approach, and they would need to learn the skills necessary to handle their new roles and responsibilities. This book represents my best ideas, using research to inform my practice, about how we can help our students learn effectively in a learner-centered classroom.

The first four chapters focus on the importance of creating clear rationales for moving from a teacher-centered to a learner-centered practice and what this means for students. It is simply human nature for our students to want to know why things have changed and how those changes will affect them. This includes *why* we want them to collaborate often but also work on their own at times; *why* we are asking them to teach each other, evaluate each other, and evaluate themselves; and *why* we are asking for so much feedback about what and how they are learning. It also explains *why* we now give cumulative exams and reflective journal assignments, and *why* we make so much of the students' work public. We cannot forget that most of our students come from a very traditional, teacher-centered learning environment, and to get them fully engaged in these new learning practices, we must continually help them to understand *why* we are asking them to change, and become significantly more involved in their learning experience.

The last eight chapters focus on the skills our students will need to learn or improve if they are to be effective learners in this new environment. They include learning on one's own; creating meaningful learning when working with others; taking more control over their learning; learning how to teach other students; becoming better presenters and performers of their learning; developing the abilities to be lifelong learners; and learning how to self-evaluate, how to evaluate others, and how to give meaningful feedback about their learning to others, including the teacher.

Most important, this book has been written to answer the single most-asked question I hear when I'm working with faculty groups: How do I help my students adjust to a learner-centered practice? I hope it offers some good answers.

I

OPTIMIZING STUDENTS' LEARNING

Many people who had difficulty in school might have prospered in their learning had the new ideas about effective instructional practices been available at the time. Furthermore, even those who did well in traditional educational environments might have developed skills, knowledge, and attitudes that would have significantly enhanced their achievements (Bransford et al., 2000, p. 5).

I began my teaching career as a reading teacher in 1972. In 1974, I was hired as a reading consultant for a rural northern Michigan school district. In this position I had the wonderful opportunity to take part in a yearlong development program for teachers of reading sponsored by the state of Michigan. This program, called The Right to Read, brought together reading consultants and teachers from across Michigan to work with leading researchers and practitioners of the reading process.

One of the first people who visited with our group had spent a great deal of his life working in adult literacy programs. As a young reading consultant, I had an interest in adult literacy and was looking forward to hearing about how to help adults learn to read. I was especially interested in discovering what specific reading techniques and materials I should use. My mind was filled with the teacher-centered questions that a young teacher working in 1974 often asked.

But instead of talking about strategies and materials, the speaker spent most of his time talking about the powerful changes that occur in families when the family leader transitions from being dependent on other family members for his or her literacy needs to no longer needing them. He talked about how important it was to teach families how to adjust to this new kind of independence. I had never stopped to think that a good deed like bringing literacy to an adult could in fact have significant effects on the person's family members, some of which might be difficult to adjust to. This powerful lesson of how one person's desire for self-improvement can affect so many other people has remained etched in my memory. What I learned from this lesson I have ingrained in my teaching, and, whenever I think about changing my teaching methods, I know that I first need to consider the implications for my students and what help they might need to adjust to the changes.

When we consider changing our teaching, there are many questions we need to ask beyond the very important question, Does the new approach enhance students' learning? For example, when a teacher decides that he or she is going to begin using small groups, the teacher needs to consider how this change will affect the students. Questions such as the following all need to be answered if the group work is to be successful, regardless of what the research says about how group work can benefit learning:

- Do the students understand why I want them to learn in small groups?
- Do they know how to work together in small groups?
- Do they know how to communicate with each other without my guiding the interaction?
- Are they able to figure out on their own what roles each member is to play in the group?

Learning how to help our students adjust to the changes that a learner-centered teaching approach requires of them is the central purpose of this book. As faculty members who have adopted a learner-centered approach to teaching, we must be willing to help our students become successful learners in a learner-centered environment. For most of our students, this learner-centered environment will be a significant departure from their earlier learning experiences, and they will not be able to adjust to it on their own. It will disrupt the expectations of schooling that have become hard-wired in their brains over the previous 12–16 years. It will change their responsibilities and their roles by asking them to take on many of the functions for which the teacher used to be responsible. These role changes will also represent more work for students.

In *Redesigning Higher Education* (1994), Gardiner points out "that if our students do not understand the learning process—the chief engine of education—they are not going to learn very much in our courses no matter what we do. One of the most valuable actions we could take to improve learning—and thus the productivity of both our students and our institutions—would be to teach our students how to learn." Gardiner's recommendation gains even more importance and greater validity in a learner-centered environment, where the traditional roles of students change dramatically. In this chapter and throughout this book, I detail the new learning roles and responsibilities that students face in a learner-centered classroom. I also describe specific ways that faculty can help students adjust to these new roles in which learning is more than listening to lectures, taking notes, and passing tests.

Teaching Is Difficult Work

I wish to begin by acknowledging a simple fact: teaching is difficult work. It is especially difficult for higher education faculty, because so few of us have had any formal development in teaching practice. However, it is difficult for *all* educators, regardless of experience or training, because we have little control over many of the very important aspects of students' lives that significantly affect their learning. For example, teachers have little control over the academic backgrounds their students bring to their courses, including the depth and breadth of their knowledge of the subject area, their critical-thinking skills, their ability to transfer knowledge from one context to another, and their abilities to organize information and study effectively. Additionally, teachers have little control over the social and emotional factors that affect students' learning, such as students' interest in a subject, their motivation for learning, their life goals, their family life, their personal health, and their finances. If this were not enough, a college professor teaching a three-credit course has only 1.7% of his or her students' time each week in which to teach them the History of Western Civilization or the Principles of Macro Economics. Teaching is not just challenging; it is difficult.

Here is another simple fact: teachers can positively impact students' learning, and highly skilled teachers can impact students' learning to even greater extents (Berry, 2005, p. 290). Despite all of the potential factors that, on any given day, can negatively affect students' learning, teachers who know how to create community, engage students actively in their learning, make content challenging and interesting, teach students how to learn the content, give students choices about what and how they learn, and make the learning meaningful, do positively affect students' learning. The methods and strategies we as teachers choose, our demonstrated passion for teaching, our skills in connecting with our students on a social and an emotional level, and our ability to teach students the learning skills they need to master the content, all of which come together to form the main focus of this book, have a direct and measurable effect on students' learning. All teaching is not equal.

Optimizing Students' Learning

Throughout this book I stress the need to create learning opportunities that optimize students' learning. This is what effective teaching does; it creates the greatest opportunity for students to learn the skills and acquire the knowledge our college and university faculty have identified as most important for them to know.

How does one go about becoming a highly skilled teacher who optimizes students' opportunities for learning? A good starting point is to heed Barr and Tagg's (1995) main message in "From Teaching to Learning." They state that teachers would be much more effective if, instead of focusing on their teaching, they focused on how and what their students are learning. In other words, we need to adopt a learner-centered approach to teaching.

Although you are probably well aware of the general concept of learner-centered teaching, let me clarify what I mean by offering this definition: Learner-centered teaching means subjecting every teaching activity (method, assignment, or assessment) to the test of a single question: "Given the context of my students, course, and classroom, will this teaching action optimize my students' opportunity to learn?"

Optimizing learning opportunities for 200 students is likely to be different from doing so for 20, so the context of the course plays a significant role in the actions a teacher can take. I choose the word *opportunities* because that is all any teacher can provide for his or her students. Great teachers maximize the opportunities for students to learn, but even the greatest teachers cannot guarantee learning. The final outcome of what is learned in any course will always be the students' responsibility.

The aforementioned simple but powerful question asks us to rethink each and every aspect of our course planning and decision making to determine whether it will optimize our students' learning opportunities. For example, if an instructor usually gives three exams and a cumulative final as the only measures for assigning grades, using that question, he or she might ask: Is the use of three exams and a final the best way to find out what my students have learned? Is it the optimal way for each student to show me what he or she knows? Are there better forms of evaluation that would promote students' learning and give summative feedback? Do these exams promote long-term learning of this material? Each of these questions represents a slightly different aspect of optimizing students' learning. All of them address the purpose of evaluations, focus on their effectiveness, and offer prompt thinking about the best way to do evaluation. The most important thing about these questions is that the act of reflecting on whether a given teaching action is the best way to optimize students' learning is a starting point for improving the opportunity for learning. The reasons for using three exams and a final often have to do with convenience for the instructor, few complaints from students, and precedent. None of these reasons meets the challenge of optimizing students' learning.

Teaching for Long-Term Learning

An equally important part of the question of whether an action optimizes students' opportunities for learning is how we define the word *learning*. There is little disagreement today that a basic definition of learning is "a change in the neural networks in the brain" (Ratey, 2002). In his book, *The Executive Brain*, Goldberg (2002) gives a more technical explanation: "When the organism is exposed to a new pattern of signals from the outside world, the strengths of synaptic contacts (the ease of signal passage between neurons) and local biochemical and electric properties gradually change in complex distributed constellations. This represents learning, as we understand it today" (p. 29). Or for those of us who are not neuroscientists, when new information is connected with what students already know, their brains develop a new network that represents that information.

However, the value and use of this new learning (these complex distributed constellations of neurons) to students depends on a multitude of factors, including, most important, how often these neurons, which are now connected, are fired (used). The extent to which these new complex distributed constellations of neurons (the new network) will become part of learners' long-term memory, and can be used to solve problems and create new knowledge, depends a great deal on how often the teacher creates opportunities for his or her students to exercise their new networks. Each time a network of neurons is fired, the potential to be fired again is increased. The long-lasting enhancement in communication between neurons, also known as *long-term potentiation*, is the reason that students who review their textbook readings or class notes daily have much greater recall potential for that information than do those who review rarely or not at all. Use it or lose it is the standard for building long-term recall of course information (Ratey, 2002, p. 17).

The learning we should be interested in helping to develop in our students is learning that is long-lasting, useful, applicable, and transferable. The definition of learning that has guided my own teaching and work in faculty development for the past 10 years is "learning is the ability to use information after significant periods of disuse and the ability to use information to solve problems that arise in a context different (if only slightly) from the context in which the information was originally learned" (Bjork, 1994, p. 187). According to this definition, learning has not occurred unless students can recall the information when they need it, later in the course or in future life activities. For example, having information for a test, at that moment, is not the same thing as having learned the information for long-term use. Testing that measures just short-term recall does a disservice to students by giving them a false sense of competence (Bjork, 1994, p. 186). In chapter 3, I discuss how using cumulative exams can help prevent students from learning material only for the test.

Also, under this definition of learning, learning has taken place only if students can transfer the information from one context to another and apply it in a useful way to solve problems and construct new understandings. Learning is not just absorbing information; it is the ability to use it. Teaching our courses with the goal of meeting the standard of this definition of learning will require helping students to learn new skills and strategies most do not currently possess. As I discuss in chapter 2, most students' previous schooling has not prepared them to engage in this kind of learning.

Engaging Students in Firsthand Learning

Learner-centered teaching can optimize students' opportunities to learn in many different ways. I have identified four specific aspects of learner-centered practice that are crucial to achieving this optimization. In the following sections, I discuss each of these aspects.

Involving Students in Firsthand Learning

The first aspect of learner-centered teaching that can optimize learning is its focus on involving students in as much firsthand learning as possible. Many college students believe that much of the work that goes into their learning should be done by the teacher. This is not surprising as this has been their experience for much of their previous education. The students' mantra of "tell me what you want me to know and I will learn it and give it back to you" is alive and thriving in higher education today. But this mantra does not lead to optimal opportunities to learn.

When students engage in firsthand learning experiences, they learn to figure things out for themselves, to believe in the analytical abilities of their own minds, to directly connect with the world around them, and to learn to use their innate curiosity to discover the power of their own learning abilities (First Hand Learning Inc., 2007). However, this powerful process is one with which students have limited familiarity, and they will need our help to learn how to be successful firsthand learners. How we as faculty can help them to value and deal effectively with firsthand learning experiences is discussed in chapter 5.

Giving Students Choices About and Control of Their Learning

The second aspect, which goes to the heart of learner-centered practice, is to share more control over students' learning with them. Sometimes we in education forget that it is indeed the students' learning we are trying to facilitate—it is, in fact, all about them.

Zull (2002), in *The Art of Changing the Brain*, explains that the brain uses four things to survive: cognition, fear, pleasure, and control (p. 51). For example, the need to have some control over what is happening in our lives is basic to being human. Schooling in America, to a great extent, has been about teachers controlling almost every aspect of students' lives. Borrowing an idea from Weimer's book, *Learner-Centered Teaching* (2002), for the past three years I have been asking faculty as I work with them at conferences or on their campuses to indicate on the list of teaching decisions provided in figure 1.1 who controls or makes the decision about how each item will be used in their courses. The choices for who controls or makes the decision are Teacher, Students, and Together. It is very unusual to find more than a few people in each session who indicate that they let students decide how the items will be used, or they make joint decisions for even 30% of the items,

FIGURE 1.1
Example form for determining who makes teaching decisions.

T = Teacher S = Students TO = Together NA = NA

1. Course textbook

2. Number of exams

3. When in the course exams will be given

4. Attendance policy

5. Late-work policy

6. Late-for-class policy

7. Course learning outcomes

8. Office hours

9. Due dates for major papers

10. Teaching methods/approaches

11. How groups are formed

12. Topic of writing or research projects

13. Grading scale

14. Discussion guidelines for large- or small-group discussions

15. Rubrics for evaluation of self or peers' work

although for at least 70–80% of the items, the decision could be shared easily without radically altering the authority or power in the classroom.

Giving students some say in their own learning is just common sense. Having a say in important aspects of our lives gives us a greater sense of control, which leads to a greater sense of safety, a greater trust in those in charge, and a willingness to be more active participants in the process. Certainly, what a student learns in college would rank as an important aspect of his or her life.

Having said all of this, students will be at different stages of readiness to take control of their learning. Many will be entering into uncharted territory and will need help to learn how to play a more active role in their own learning, which will include learning how to take on new responsibilities and roles that previously belonged to the teacher. They will need our guidance to understand why these new roles and responsibilities will improve their learning and how they'll need to adapt their thinking and change their behavior to take them on.

Teaching Students Lifelong Learning Skills

> The illiterate of the 21st century will not be those who cannot read and write, but those who cannot learn, unlearn, and relearn.
>
> —Alvin Toffler (1970)

The third aspect of a learner-centered practice goes hand-in-hand with teaching for long-term memory. As an integrated part of teaching our course content, we need to teach the lifelong learning skills that our students will need to live successfully in an ever-expanding global economy. Development of these skills is often lacking, as demonstrated by the following statement, which I use to begin every one of my presentations to faculty:

> Not a single employment recruiter or graduate school admission recruiter has ever said, "What we are looking for in a college graduate is someone who is great at note taking and excels on multiple-choice tests."

The obvious point is that the skills students need for lifelong learning are often not the skills they spend a great deal of time practicing in college. I have yet to find anyone in higher education who contests that students today are facing ever-expanding amounts of knowledge that cannot be taught in any reasonable time frame, much less in the 1.7% of the time each week most instructors (three-credit courses) have to teach their courses. The Association of Research Libraries estimated that 600,000 new books were published worldwide in 1999. There is more and more to know, and the amount of time college students are given to learn this knowledge has not changed in hundreds of years (Smith, 2004, p. xix).

Most faculty recognize that it is no longer possible to teach all of the things they so strongly feel students need to know. Most of us also recognize, but find it harder to accept, that the knowledge and skills we have worked so hard to learn ourselves cannot be shared with students in only three hours a week. Nobel laureate Herbert Simon (1996) put it this way: "The meaning of knowing has shifted from being able to remember and repeat information to being able to find and use it. The goal of education is better conceived as helping students develop the intellectual tools and learning strategies needed to acquire the knowledge necessary to think productively."

One of the main aspects of a learner-centered practice is to prepare students for their future learning (Weimer, 2002, p. 5). To optimize this preparation, we need to help our students develop lifelong learning skills that include the learning-how-to-learn skills and strategies needed to deal with the complex and challenging subject matter they will encounter in college and beyond.

These learning-how-to-learn skills typically go beyond the learning strategies most students have in their repertoire. Skills such as how to locate needed information, how to evaluate the source of that information, how to collaborate with others to create meaningful learning, how to solve problems found in contexts different from those with which they are familiar, how to organize information into meaningful patterns, and how to think in the specific ways of a subject discipline are all skills that most college students do not adequately possess and, therefore, need to learn. To believe that students should somehow intuitively have learned these skills or that they had been taught them elsewhere but had forgotten them is fantasy. If they are to learn these skills, we will have to teach them.

In working with faculty groups I always pose the following question: What would make you happy or satisfied that your students still knew, from all of the knowledge and skills you taught in a given course, six months after the course was completed? The most common answer I get is that they would be happy if their students retained certain main concepts and specific learning and thinking skills that would help prepare them for their next course in the sequence or for their long-term future learning (lifelong learning). In addition, many faculty respond that the question helps them decide, from this ever-expanding amount of knowledge, what to include in their courses. Only rarely do faculty answer "everything" or recite a specific list of facts or definitions. One of the most important aspects of learner-centered teaching is that its focus includes preparing students for their future learning.

Promoting the Relevance of Learner-Centered Teaching

The fourth aspect of successfully implementing a learner-centered practice is to be able to explain to students why you want them to change their roles and responsibilities, and how these changes will produce deeper and long-lasting learning. In his 2000 book, *The Tipping Point*, Malcolm Gladwell writes about the incredible amount of research that went into the development of the TV program, *Sesame Street*, in particular, the time spent trying to understand which elements of the show made children pay attention and which caused them to lose interest. One of the fascinating findings was that the children lost interest not because the colors were not bright enough or the characters attractive, but when they did not understand what was going on. We should take this lesson from *Sesame Street* to heart. Students might lose interest in what we are trying to teach because they do not understand why the information is important or relevant to their lives or to the learning goals of the class. Or it might be that they do not understand how the information can be applied in any meaningful way, or why the particular way the professor is requesting the information be learned is necessary or the best way to learn it.

To optimize students' opportunities to learn, we must first present a clear rationale for learning the skills and information presented in our courses. This will enable our students to decide whether it is worthwhile for them to engage in learning. Zull (2002) states, "If people believe it is important to their lives they will learn" (p. 52). This topic is more fully explored in chapter 3.

The Traditional Roles and Responsibilities of College Learners

As we observe the students sitting in our college classrooms today, it is easy to identify differences between them and earlier generations. We can see for ourselves the changes in hairstyles, fashion, and attitudes toward piercing and tattoos. However, what have changed little in the past 250 years are the assumptions about the respective roles and responsibilities of teachers and students in the higher education learning process (Smith, 2004). Smith put it this way: "At Yale or Yakima, backpack wearing students absorb knowledge from someone wiser, regurgitate that knowledge to the wiser person's satisfaction, receive grades and move on to sit in more classes, absorb knowledge from someone wiser and so on" (p. xviii).

What do college students think is expected of them as learners in today's college classrooms? That is a very easy question to answer: the same roles they had in high school. Although they know college will be harder, and they know they will be asked to study more, they do not expect any substantive changes in their classroom roles. They have learned from their high school experiences that skills such as note taking, highlighting, organizing, summarizing, outlining, listening, and memorizing are vital to their academic success. They have learned that the teacher does most of the talking, and that the textbook contains a great deal of the test material. They may have learned the basics of doing presentations and how to manage an out-of-class project, and they may have done some collaborative learning. They also do not anticipate these basic roles to change much as they enter college.

What a surprise it is to students when a teacher adopts a learner-centered practice. Students often become very uncomfortable and even hostile toward the new roles and responsibilities they are being asked to take on, for two primary reasons. First, these new roles do not, from their perspective, fit their idea of what school should be like. The roles do not match the patterns for student learning they recognize. Second, they see the teacher as abdicating his or her responsibilities as the giver of knowledge, and they do not understand where the knowledge and skills they are expected to learn will come from. Some faculty with whom I have worked offer a third reason for their students' dismay: the students do not think they are getting their money's worth unless the teacher is controlling the classroom and doing the talking.

The major learning roles and responsibilities most often associated with traditional learning, listed in figure 1.2, represent what the great majority of

FIGURE 1.2
Major traditional learning roles and responsibilities.

Roles	*Responsibilities*
• Take lecture notes. • Listen in class. • Read the textbook. • Read other assigned reading. • Take tests and quizzes. • Take part in recitation.	• Work mostly alone. • Seek out the teacher if you have questions. • Read independently. • Develop your own study habits. • Develop your own time-management program. • Organize the information. • Write papers on assigned topics. • Memorize.

college undergraduates expect to do to be successful in college. You may be able to add to this list, but it is fairly representative of traditional classroom learning.

To many of us, the roles and responsibilities in the list are the same ones we had as learners in college 10, 20, or more years ago. Clearly we did just fine. Consequently, some of you may ask, What is the big deal with learner-centered teaching? My response to this question is that most of us did well because we were bright and motivated enough to teach ourselves much of the course information despite the teacher-centered learning environment. Many successful college graduates learned in spite, not because, of their teachers.

However, the big deal about learner-centered teaching is that, although these traditional roles worked for us when we were in college decades ago, they did not work well for half of the college students of our day, and they work even less well today. Continuing to rely on (teacher-centered) methods flies in the face of what we know about how people learn and our historical record of failure with a rapidly diversifying population (Smith, 2004, p. xix). Table 1.1 looks at graduation rates from 1983 to 1997. Note a slow but steady decline in the number of students graduating over a 5-year period and that nearly half of the entering students did not graduate within 5 years.

College graduation rates have increased slightly in the past 5 years, with the National Center for Education Statistics reporting a 2004 graduation rate of 57% (Horn, 2006).

New Roles and Responsibilities for Students

As an example of the kind of deep learning that can come from a learner-centered approach, let's explore what happens to the learning process when

TABLE 1.1
Graduation rates* at four-year colleges and universities

	1983	*1985*	*1986*	*1987*	*1988*	*1989*	*1990*	*1991*	*1992*	*1993*	*1994*	*1995*	*1996*	*1997*
Public	52.2	51.2	49.9	48.5	48.0	48.2	47.9	46.6	46.7	46.3	45.6	46.1	44.6	**44.2**
Private	59.5	58.4	58.4	58.4	58.1	58.0	57.8	57.7	57.6	57.7	57.2	57.5	57.1	**56.6**
All	57.5	56.3	56.0	55.5	55.2	55.1	54.9	54.4	54.4	54.3	53.7	54.0	53.3	**52.8**

*Percentage of students graduating within five years. Record lows are in boldface; 1984 data are unavailable.
Source: ACT News, 1998

a teacher asks a student to teach some information or a skill to other students. Implicit in this request is that the student doing the teaching will need an in-depth understanding of the information or the skill for his or her teaching to be effective. The process will likely cause the student to undertake reading and research and to analyze and evaluate the material to determine the key concepts that his or her classmates will need to learn. The student will also need to find images or analogies to help the class understand the material. Finally, the student will need to anticipate classmates' questions and decide how to involve the other students in learning the information and how to assess whether they have learned. In addition, the teacher will ask the student audience to be prepared to give feedback to the student teacher on what they learned and the effectiveness of the presentation by using a rubric. The student teacher may also ask the students to complete an assessment, such as a quiz or summary paper, and be prepared to be questioned about the accuracy of the information that he or she presented or the conclusions drawn. This example illustrates how changing the role of the learner results in a learning process that richly deepens the student teacher's understanding of the course material and simultaneously engages his or her peers actively in the learning.

In a learner-centered classroom students are asked to take on significantly different roles and responsibilities from those they have previously encountered. The new roles and responsibilities are not new to teaching; they are simply new to students. When these roles and responsibilities are handed over to students in reasonable and manageable ways, they create the opportunity to optimize students' learning. Not only is the depth of learning and long-term recall of the information and skills enhanced, but by letting our students explore or solve the problem on their own, or with others, many additional effective benefits result. Students engaged in discovery learning, for example, also find out how they learn best. When we give our students learning activities that require them to work on their own or collaborate with others, we create a genuine opportunity for students to experience a sense of accomplishment and empowerment from handling the task, and they develop greater confidence in their own abilities as learners.

Figure 1.3 provides a list of new roles and responsibilities students may be given in a learner-centered environment. It is not a comprehensive list, so you will probably wish to add to it based on your own teaching experiences. These new roles and responsibilities all require the students to do more work

FIGURE 1.3
Roles and responsibilities for students in a learner-centered environment.

Learner-Centered Student Roles	*Learner-Centered Student Responsibilities*
Self-teach	Make choices about one's own learning
Collaborate with others	
Work in teams/groups	Take more control of one's own learning
Take part in discovery learning	
Teach others	Give input to the evaluation/ assessment methods of the course
Evaluate own learning	
Evaluate others' learning	Give input to course rules and guidelines
Perform/present learning publicly	
Learn new how-to-learn skills and strategies	Give formative feedback on learning to peers
Solve authentic problems	Evaluate one's own learning
Engage in reflection	
Demonstrate use of teacher feedback to improve performance	Spend more time learning outside of class
Take learning risks	Work with people from outside the university on service projects or other authentic learning activities
Practice more	
Take class notes	
Listen in class	
Read the textbook	
Write papers	
Take tests and quizzes	
Take part in recitation	
Do homework	

and take on more responsibility for their learning. You will note that several of the roles listed are the same as those given for the traditional roles in figure 1.2. These learning roles continue to be of value in a learner-centered classroom when used to optimize students' learning.

If our students are to be successful in these new learning roles, they will need help and guidance from us. They will also need clear explanations why taking on these roles, which require more work and more time on their part, are in their best interest. These issues are explored in chapter 2.

Every aspect of our teaching offers us opportunities to enhance the quality, depth, and permanence of our students' learning. It requires only that we think about how each teaching choice will affect our students and whether our students will need any new skills or strategies to take full advantage of the learning opportunities we seek to provide.

2

WHY STUDENTS RESIST
LEARNER-CENTERED
TEACHING

The adoption of a learner-centered teaching approach seems, on the surface, to be something our students would embrace. It gives them more control over their learning; it offers them choices about what and how to learn, a variety of activities and assignments, and more firsthand exploratory learning opportunities; and it is more interactive. However, hundreds of faculty, both at Ferris State (where I teach) and across the country, who took part in my learner-centered workshops, found a very different reaction when introducing learner-centered methods. They reported that many students were angry and upset, and complained about the changes being implemented. This discontent occurred even though faculty started their implementation process slowly and introduced only a few changes. The reason for the hostility is the powerfully entrenched teacher-centered view of learning these students possess. The learner-centered approach looks nothing like most of their previous school experiences.

Our Biggest Challenge

The single biggest challenge we face in successfully adopting a learner-centered approach to teaching is getting our students to buy into the change, to switch their learning paradigm. The reality is that, without this acceptance, chaos and constant complaining are likely to reign in the classroom. Meeting this challenge, despite the problems some faculty have reported, is not that difficult; it just requires an effective three-step plan. Step one is to understand why our students are resistant to the roles and responsibilities of a learner-centered environment. Step two is to share with our students a clear set of reasons, backed up by research, why they need to take on new learning roles and responsibilities, even though they are content with their old ones. Step three is to teach our students the new learning skills they will need to be successful in a learner-centered classroom. This chapter is devoted to accomplishing step one. Chapters 3 and 4 provide information for accomplishing step two, and chapters 5 through 12 provide instructions for implementing step three.

Reasons for Students' Resistance

> It takes a lot of courage to release the familiar and seemingly secure, to embrace the new. But there is no real security in what is no longer meaningful. There is more security in the adventurous and exciting, for in movement there is life, and in change there is power.
>
> —Alan Cohen

As Cohen so eloquently put it, when we ask our students to adopt new roles as learners and take on new responsibilities, we are asking them to have the courage to give up some of the security and familiarity of their past learning behaviors. We are asking our students to trust us when we tell them that, even though their old learning behaviors are comfortable and may have led to much success in high school, changing these behaviors is clearly the right thing to do. To help our students accept this change, we must first understand why most will resist. I have had numerous discussions over the past four years with faculty who are working to implement a learner-centered approach, and we have jointly identified eight reasons why students resist adopting learner-centered behaviors. You may be able to add to this list, and you may see some overlap in the reasons, but the list represents the distilled experiences of many faculty:

1. Old habits die hard.
2. High schools remain teacher-centered institutions.
3. Learning is not a top reason students give for attending college.
4. Students do not like taking learning risks.
5. Learner-centered teaching does not resemble what students think of as school.

6. Students do not want to put forth the extra effort learner-centered teaching requires.
7. Students' mind-sets about learning make adapting to learner-centered teaching more difficult.
8. Many students follow the path of least resistance in their learning.

Now let's explore each of these reasons in depth.

Old Habits Die Hard

A study led by Ann Graybiel (2005) of MIT's McGovern Institute found that,

> although habits help us through the day, eliminating the need to strategize about each tiny step involved in driving to work and other complex routines, habits (especially bad habits), can have a vise grip on both mind and behavior. Important neural activity patterns in a specific region of the brain change when habits are formed, change again when habits are broken, but quickly re-emerge when something rekindles an extinguished habit— routines that originally took great effort to learn. (p. 1158)

The expectations many students have about their roles and responsibilities as college learners are based on strongly formed habits learned through 12 or more years of teacher-centered instruction. These habits include such things as sitting quietly, doing the assigned homework , taking lecture notes, and answering multiple-choice questions. After many years, school has a very familiar pattern to it.

For students to change their learning habits and have those changes remain in place, as is necessary in a learner-centered classroom, they will need significant help in understanding why the changes are necessary (see chapters 3 and 4) as well as how to make the changes (see chapters 5–12). They will also need regular reinforcement and encouragement from us.

In our students' previous learning environment, the importance of memorization was stressed, rather than the value of learning with understanding. Facts and details often were a primary focus, not the larger themes of causes and consequences. The shortfalls of these approaches are not apparent if the only test of learning involves testing memory. When the transfer of learning is measured, as is done in a learner-centered classroom, the shortfalls become very apparent (Bransford, Brown, & Cocking, 1999, p. 8). It will take our students time and a great deal of practice to develop a new set of learning habits. We should anticipate that occasionally they will fall back into their old ways, for old habits die hard.

High Schools Remain Teacher-Centered Institutions

I have a great deal of respect for my colleagues who teach in our public and private secondary schools. The teaching they do is fraught with difficult challenges, and their work is vital to the welfare of all Americans. However, the research on American high schools indicates that they are teacher-centered, not learner-centered. At the 2003 Lilly West Conference, keynote speaker Dr. Fredrick Baker (Cal-Poly Pomona) (2003), a nationally known researcher on the state of education both in the United States and abroad, told the audience that much positive, learner-centered change had occurred in the elementary schools in the United States, resulting in measurable learning gains. He went on to say that some moderate change was being seen at the middle school level as well. Unfortunately, the news about our high schools was not as good. He reported that they had not changed, and that their instructional methods are much like they were decades ago. The National Commission on the Senior Year came to a similar conclusion in 2001:

> Despite the efforts of many, the organization and structure of most comprehensive high schools look very similar to those of high schools of generations ago. High schools have stood still amidst a maelstrom of educational and economic change swirling around them. (U.S. Department of Education, 2001)

Because our high schools have not changed, it is fair to assume that our students will expect to use their high school learning habits when they enter college. Our students are most likely to maintain a simple philosophy: if it isn't broken, don't fix it. Many of our students were highly successful in their teacher-centered high school courses and have no reason to think the same habits that got them As in high school, and high scores on the ACT or the SAT, will not work in college. We should not be surprised by this, for it is a logical conclusion for them to reach. Nor should we expect high schools to embrace the learner-centered paradigm anytime soon. If our students are to change, we will have to be the facilitators of that change.

Learning Is Not a Top Reason Students Give for Attending College

In his 10-year study of high school students, Steinberg (1997) reported that the most common reason students gave for trying in school was not interest in the subject, but getting good grades so they could get into college. Perhaps even more disconcerting is the finding of a study by Levine and Cureton (1998) that 37% of students would drop out of college if they thought college was not helping their chances of getting a job (p. 116). By age 18, many students are sick to death of school and just see college as the last hurdle to be crossed (Leamnson, 1999, p. 35).

These findings are not all that surprising. During the 20 years I taught teacher-centered critical reading courses (1977–1998), I regularly made notes from students' evaluations in hopes of recognizing patterns in my teaching that I could change to improve it. On these evaluations, I asked students what they liked and what they did not like about the course. Figure 2.1 presents edited versions of the most common responses. My students' views of learning are quite consistent with what one might expect from students educated in a teacher-centered system. They also shed light on why students may struggle to adapt to the new roles and responsibilities that are asked of them in a learner-centered classroom. In addition, the responses often reflect Steinberg's findings that school is about surface things such as grades, tests, workload, and how students feel about the teacher. The students did not write about what they learned, or how they were challenged to change their thinking, or how better prepared they were for future college courses—all

FIGURE 2.1
Common student responses to a Critical Reading course evaluation.

There was too much homework.
I didn't like that we had to take so many notes in class.
We had too much reading to do in this class. The teacher should give us less.
I didn't like that we had essay tests. The teacher should give us multiple-choice tests.
The teacher was really nice—I liked him.
The teacher made the assignments very clear.
The teacher spent a lot of time trying to get someone to answer the questions he asked.
I think the teacher should give us points for discussion.
A lot of the work seemed like busywork.
I liked that we could get extra credit.
The course was too easy—I didn't learn very much. The teacher needs to challenge us more.
I liked the stories the teacher told, but not all the writing we had to do.
I wish my other teachers were more interested in us like this teacher is.

goals I had for the course. The consistency of the responses over such a long period led me to conclude that students see school in terms of work to get out of the way, not learning to be embraced.

Students Do Not Like Taking Learning Risks

Thomas Edison failed more than 3,000 times to find the material that would eventually become the filament for the lightbulb. When asked about it, he responded that he hadn't failed, that he had eliminated from the search thousands of things that did not work. Unfortunately, this positive view of taking risks and learning from failure is not the dominant mind-set of most college students. Teachers know that learning anything entails taking some risks and confronting the possibility of failure. But as we grow older, we develop a tendency to hide from failure (Tagg, 2003, p. 54). Students who see failure as an enemy to be avoided can feel a sense of helplessness in potential learning situations, leading to the very failure they hope to avoid. When this failure occurs repeatedly, it will inhibit their learning (Dweck, 2000). Students who do not take risks or make mistakes—the very actions in which successful thinkers must engage—are in the business of protecting their unblemished record of mediocrity (Covington, 1992, p. 231). Despite growing up as risk takers, many students fail to maintain a willingness to take risks in a school environment.

A great example of students avoiding learning risks developed in the honors program at Ferris State in 1998. I received a call from the program coordinator concerning a problem that several of the honors faculty were having with the lack of student participation in classroom discussions. The honors faculty believed that, as the best and brightest at Ferris State, these students should have been exchanging ideas, challenging each other, and sharing their insights, but this was not occurring. The coordinator's question was, How could the honors faculty get the students to participate more fully in class discussions?

I suggested that perhaps the students were avoiding discussion because their previous learning experiences taught them that if they could get an A without taking the risk of speaking up in class, then they would be crazy to say anything. By speaking up in class, honors students, in particular, run the risk that if they make a mistake, that error will reveal that they might not be as smart as they want their peers to think they are. An even worse scenario would be for their teachers to discover that they are not as smart as they want them to think they are. Many students hope to avoid public failure or embarrassment by remaining silent. They view speaking out, which creates the possibility of giving a wrong answer or an answer with which others may disagree, as just not worth it unless a grade is at stake. Students have learned from 12 or more years of school that the important thing is the grade. Therefore, the path of least risk to obtaining that grade is the one to take.

The honors students were simply practicing what they had learned throughout their schooling: don't do any more than is necessary to get the A. In his book, *Punished by Rewards*, Kohn (1993) describes classrooms as economies in which students do not do any learning without some corresponding "pay." Accordingly, learning is not seen as having value in and of itself; it is only a means to an end, which is the grade. If a grade is not at stake, as is often the case in discussions, why bother? Getting our students to abandon this highly ingrained mentality is not easy.

The answer I gave the honors coordinator was to tell the faculty to make class participation a meaningful part of the students' final grade. This action would demonstrate to the students that the teachers valued discussion. By changing the rules so the students could not get an A without participating, the faculty were using the students' "grade obsession" as a means of getting them to take part in class discussions. It was my hope that the students would discover that active participation in discussions is a great way to learn and can be emotionally, socially, and intellectually rewarding.

If I had answered the honors coordinator's question in 2007, my answer would have been quite different. I would have suggested the honors faculty use the approach I am detailing in this book. They should establish a rationale for the use of discussion in college learning. This would include explaining why class participation is a vital element of students' learning, that discussions unlock the intellectual diversity of each member of the class and allow all members to learn from one another's ideas. The faculty should also present research findings demonstrating that discussion easily surpasses lecture as a deep learning process (Terenzini, Cabrera, Colbeck, Parente, & Bjorklund, 2001) and leads to the examination of diverse viewpoints, helps with the discovery of new ways to solve problems, trains us to speak clearly and concisely, and teaches us how to listen to others and give meaningful feedback. In addition, the faculty should explain to the students that, because most professionals spend their workdays discussing issues with clients, patients, customers, colleagues, and bosses, speaking and listening are among the most important skills they need to develop; if they cannot speak and listen effectively, their careers can be negatively affected. In addition, I would have told the coordinator that the faculty would need to teach the students how to engage in effective discussion, because most students are not well versed in these skills.

The lesson I learned from the honors students is that students need good reasons to take learning risks. This is a lesson we will all need to remember as we implement a learner-centered practice.

Learner-Centered Teaching Does Not Resemble What Students Think of as School

By age 18, our students have spent 70% of their lives in school (Leamnson, 1999, p. 35), with each school year looking a great deal like the one before. Our students know school is most often a place where the teacher does the talking and the students do the listening, note taking, completing of worksheets, and test taking. They know their teachers' communication with them most often takes the form of directions, such as, "Sit down and be quiet" and "Turn in your homework." Students also know school as a place where they are often given time to do their homework in class and effort is rewarded with a passing grade. The learning choices students are given are usually limited and may include selecting the topic or book they would like to write about. Basically they must do their work and pass, or not do their work and fail. The only area of real control students have over their learning is the degree to which they choose to engage in the learning process, but even that control is limited, because if they choose not to engage in learning, they must suffer the consequences.

It is easy to understand why students who have never experienced a learning environment where meaningful control and choices about learning were offered, or where opportunities for firsthand learning existed, would be tentative, cautious, and uncomfortable in a learner-centered environment. It is also not surprising that these students would be upset by a learning approach where the role of the teacher has changed so much that it appears as if the teacher is not doing his or her job.

From many students' perspective, if the teacher is not talking, then he or she is not teaching. The teacher as facilitator is a role college students rarely see their teachers playing. I can recall a time in my early teaching career when I first began using small groups, and one of my students said to me as he was leaving the classroom, "So you didn't feel like teaching today." At that time, many students had not been exposed to group learning and did not understand its value or why it would be an effective way for them to learn. They did not view group learning as a useful learning tool. I soon realized that I had not prepared my students for learning in groups, that I had thought they would figure it out on their own, which, of course, they did not.

Another common student reaction to a learner-centered environment in higher education is that students feel that, since they are paying for their education, the teacher should be doing the teaching. They should not have to "help" the teacher do his or her job. There is a clear disconnect between what we want them to do in a learner-centered classroom and what they see as their role in the learning process.

Students Do Not Want to Put Forth the Extra Effort Learner-Centered Teaching Requires

Faculty often hear students complain that learner-centered teaching requires more work. This observation by our students is correct. I regularly tell faculty that it is the *one who does the work, who does the learning*. Our students will be asked to do more firsthand work, more teamwork and group work, more research and investigation, more reflection, and more talking and listening. All of these learning activities require a certain amount of effort; they are not passive, sit-there-and-listen activities.

Cross (2001), in discussing American students' views about effort, states, "One of the oddities of traditional American culture, especially the youth culture, is that it is better to be thought lazy than stupid. Thus, in the competition of the classroom, students prefer to be seen by others as succeeding through ability rather than through effort." In other words, giving more effort is disdained not only because it means more work but also because in our American culture many students believe if you have to work at learning, you must not be very smart. I explore this view of effort, part of a larger view of learning that students take with them as they develop their own self-theories about learning, more fully later in this chapter.

There are certainly other reasons why students do not see the need to use effort unless it is absolutely necessary. One is the use of extrinsic motivators, which often cause students to do as little as possible. This is discussed later in this chapter. Another effort inhibitor is the sense of pride some students take in doing the least amount of work possible and still earning a good grade. I call this the efficiency of effort model. A great example of this came from my own 16-year-old son. He is an excellent student but, more important, a genuinely curious, investigative, and self-motivated learner. He recently told me that he is going to read *A Walk in the Woods* by Bill Bryson (1999) for his first book report in his literature class. This is his all-time favorite book, a book he has read twice and listened to on tape three times. When I asked if he thought it might be better to expand his reading horizons and choose a book he had not read, he replied, "When the opportunity comes along to use very little effort to accomplish a major assignment in a class, you have to take advantage of it." He then added, "I have a lot of work in my other classes, plus golf practice, so I would be stupid not to take advantage of this." His philosophy of effort was: only use it when you have to. In truth, however, this efficiency of effort view, although appearing to make good sense, just detracts from learning.

For example, the conclusion of almost all of those who research the topic of greatness find that greatness is to a greater extent the result of hard work and effort, and more hard work (Colvin, 2006). If our students are to succeed both in college and beyond, one of the greatest gifts we could give them is to help them improve their efforts to learn.

Students' Mind-Sets About Learning Make Adapting to Learner-Centered Teaching More Difficult

Thousands of students each semester pay tuition to take courses in subject areas they firmly believe they cannot learn. This belief results from the fixed mind-set that these students have developed about learning a particular subject (Dweck, 2006).[1] Students with a fixed mind-set view intelligence and ability as fundamentally fixed at birth and unchangeable. These students see themselves and others as smart, average, or dumb. They spend a great deal of effort trying to prove that they are "smart" by avoiding failure, which

---

1. It should be noted that Dweck has found that a mind-set can change from domain to domain, for example, extracurricular activities versus academic activities, and people can be taught to develop a new mind-set.

actually prevents them from engaging in activities that, ironically, would make them smarter. When it comes to certain school subjects, a student with a fixed mind-set believes you either get it or you don't. The majority of college students have this fixed mind-set toward some of their subjects (Covington, 1992). This is also the perspective of most high school students (Steinberg, 1997).

A fixed mind-set has a profound impact on students' views of a variety of learning-related actions. For example, students may see expending effort in certain learning activities as being of little or no use. In addition, students may view tutoring, study buddies, or visits to our offices for extra help a waste of time. Helping our students to replace their false beliefs about learning capacity with an understanding that effort, time, and effective teaching can result in success in any subject, is crucial to optimizing their learning opportunities. It is one of the most important actions we can take to help our students be successful. As Alfred Binet (1911) said nearly a hundred years ago, it is not always the people who start out the smartest who end up the smartest.

The opposite of a fixed mind-set is the growth mind-set. Students with a growth mind-set believe that "your basic qualities are things you can cultivate through your efforts" (Dweck, 2006, p. 7). They believe that "a person's true potential is unknown (and unknowable); that it's impossible to foresee what can be accomplished with years of passion, toil and training" (p. 7). These students take learning risks and view failure only as a message that they need to figure out what they did wrong and work harder to improve. In *Mindset* (2006), Dweck relates an experiment that she conducted with high-ability college students that gets to the heart of how a mind-set affects a person's view of himself or herself as a learner. Students were given a scenario in which, first, they earn only a C+ on a midterm paper; second, they get a parking ticket; and, finally, when they go to share their bad day with their best friend, they get the brush-off. Dweck reported that those with fixed mind-sets reacted with very personal negative statements about these events. Responses included "I feel like a reject," "I'm a failure," and "I'm an idiot." By contrast, the students with a growth mind-set reacted with comments, such as, "I need to try harder in class and watch where I park my car," "I would start studying harder," and "I would pay the ticket and work things out with my friend." According to Dweck, in a growth mind-set, it is not that people do not get upset about parking tickets or a bad grade; it is that they do not see these occurrences as defining who they are or as threatening their intelligence. They try to learn from their mistakes and move on (p. 8).

The mind-set of students also has a significant impact on the kinds of goals they set as learners. There is general agreement that students may set two types of goals. One is a learning goal, which is described as the desire to increase one's competency, understanding, and appreciation of what is being learned. The other is a performance goal, which involves outperforming others as a means to aggrandizing one's ability status at the expense of one's peers (Covington, 2000). Or, to put it another way, a performance goal setter wants to look good by making others look bad.

The specific hypothesis put forward by those who study this area is twofold: First, learning goals favor deep-level, strategic processing of information, leading to increased school achievement, greater pride and satisfaction in learning successes, and a better ability to handle failure if it occurs (Ames, 1992; Jagacinski & Nicholls, 1984, 1987). Second, performance goals trigger superficial, rote-level processing that exerts a stultifying influence on achievement (Covington, 2000, p. 173). Performance goals are about getting positive judgments of your competence and avoiding negative ones, while learning goals are about increasing your competency (Dweck, 2000, p. 15). Learning goals and performance goals are not mutually exclusive; a student can value the task itself, as well as the outcome of the task (Hagen & Weinstein, 1995).

In *Self-Theories,* Dweck (2000) states that students tend to value one goal over another, though which goals they set may differ in different domains of activity. However, it is important to note that when students have a fixed mind-set, they are more likely to set performance goals in an academic setting (p. 18).

Additionally, as stated earlier, students who see failure as an enemy to be avoided may become helpless in learning situations, and when this response occurs repeatedly, it will inhibit learning (Dweck, 2000, p. 26). One of the most important findings for all college teachers to remember is that it is possible to positively influence students' mind-sets, and when this occurs, students' learning goals can change as well (p. 26).

Many Students Follow the Path of Least Resistance in Their Learning

I regularly describe students who take the path of least resistance as minimalist learners. These are students who adhere to the philosophy, "Whatever is the least I have to do to get the grade I need is the way to go." They often ask, "How many points is this worth?" followed by, "How many points do I need to get an A, a B, or a C?" These questions reflect a lifetime of learning in an environment where trying to gain a reward or avoid a punishment was the goal. The goal of minimalist learners is the grade, not the learning.

Students' motivation for learning has a big impact on what path they take as learners. Research on students' motivation to learn has recently focused on two distinct incentive systems. Covington (2000) offered this description of the first one:

> The first system assumes that students are optimally motivated by there being fewer rewards than there are players in the learning game, i.e., turning students into competitors for recognition and further advancement. This model derives much of its justification from the view of motives-as-drivers, which typically considers motivation an enabling factor, i.e., the means to superior performance. This scarcity of rewards disrupts learning by encouraging negative achievement goals, such as avoiding failure, rather than positive goals, such as striving for success. Special attention is given to the particularly devastating impact of reward scarcity on disenfranchised students and students of color, as well as on teachers themselves. (p. 172)

Regarding the second incentive system, which is viewed as an alternative to the competitive model, Covington (2000) states that it assumes that

> motivation is optimal when there exists an abundance of payoffs for learning, and payoffs of many kinds, not just tangible, extrinsic rewards like grades or gold stars, but also intrinsic sources of satisfaction, as well as a variety of ways in which to earn these rewards, ways suited to individual learning styles. This model reflects an emphasis on motives-as-goals that draw, not drive, individuals toward action, and generally for ennobling reasons: for the sake of curiosity, exploration, and self-improvement. (p. 172)

This second incentive system is an integral part of a learner-centered approach to instruction. Kohn (1993) strongly suggests that the use of rewards will likely reduce students' learning because it makes the reward, rather than the learning, the goal of the schooling process (e.g., p. 211). This narrow focus on the grade as the important outcome was brought home to me while teaching a graduate course in content area reading a few summers ago. About three weeks before the end of the course, an older adult student approached me and asked what her final grade would be if she did not do the final project. I asked her, naïvely, why she would not want to complete the course and learn as much as possible about how to help her students improve their reading skills. She replied that she was taking the course because she needed three more credits to get a pay raise at her current school, and a grade of B would be sufficient to meet the criteria set by her school district. She was using the same philosophy as my 16-year-old son: use only as much effort as needed to get the reward you are seeking. I told her that she would earn a B even without the last project. She thanked me and did not return to class for the rest of the semester.

As I reflected on this student's behavior, two things bothered me. One was my own naïveté in not making the requirement for passing the course the successful completion of all assigned projects. Learner-centered teaching is about giving students some control and choice over their learning. However, in doing so, I should not have abdicated my responsibility to prepare my students as completely as possible to be effective teachers. The second thing that bothered me was my failure to make the learning more relevant and meaningful to this student. I felt that if I had done a better job of getting her to see the value in learning all she could to help her own students, perhaps she would have attended the rest of the classes.

Now, as I think back on this incident, I realize two important things. First, even if I had done an excellent job of creating a compelling reason for learning everything that was available in the course, this student still might have opted for the low-effort route. I know that, in the end, each student will make his or her own decisions about what is important in his or her learning life. Second, minimalist behaviors are not limited to students. They are also found among faculty and contribute greatly to the continuance of a teacher-centered approach to college instruction. By choosing what is best and easiest for the teacher when making decisions about students' learning, faculty are practicing a form of minimalism. Learner-centered teaching takes more time, effort, creativity, and involvement than does teacher-centered practice, for both the students and the teacher. When we look at the work involved in optimizing our students' opportunities to learn, it is not difficult to see why some teachers are resistant to learner-centered practice for the same reason students are: it involves more work and effort. For these faculty to embrace a learner-centered approach, they will need to make both a philosophical change and a pedagogical one.

Zull (2002) makes the case that this minimalist behavior comes from the brain seeing extrinsic motivation as a "loss of control" (p. 53). According to him, the brain has evolved over 5 million years to detect and resist exactly this type of situation. He states, "In fact, one of the things the brain does best is decipher deceptions like extrinsic rewards" (p. 53). Zull is not suggesting that there is no value in the use of rewards or punishment; he acknowledges that they are useful tools to initiate interest in new areas of learning or to sustain engagement when things get tough (p. 53). The point is that, as an overall strategy for teaching and learning, the use of rewards and punishments falls far short of creating a sustainable learning environment. Our students are just too wise to how this game is played. Finally, extrinsic rewards can lead students to consider other creative ways to get the rewards, including turning in someone else's work as their own and cheating on a test as opposed to studying for it themselves. I am not making excuses for students who do these things, simply pointing out that if the goal is the grade, rather than learning, students can sometimes take a wrong turn in reaching that goal.

For Students to Change Will Take Time

Woods (1994) described the transition students go through when they are asked to enter a completely new learning format (in this case he was describing students' encounter with problem-based learning) as similar to the steps psychologists associate with trauma and grief—steps that begin with initial shock, then move on to resistance, and, finally, end with acceptance. I doubt the changes we are asking our students to make in accepting a learner-centered teaching approach are so traumatic that they will need to grieve over the loss of their old learning habits. I am certain, however, that not only will our students need clear reasons for making the changes, they will need our help to make the changes successfully, and these changes will take time. A colleague of mine shared that when he switched his teaching approach from lecturing to small-group learning in his physics course, his students did not believe there would be no lectures. It was six weeks into the semester before his students accepted the small-group model and realized that he was serious about no longer lecturing. Our students' views of what school should be and the roles teachers should play are strongly ingrained. We must help them to adjust to the learner-centered environment and give them the time they need to accept this approach to teaching and learning.

3

CREATING RELEVANCE FOR A LEARNER-CENTERED PRACTICE

"Finish your homework before you watch TV."
"*Why?*"
"Because I said so."

—Winnie Doyle

My mother's explanation about why I had to wait to watch TV was crystal clear but never fully satisfactory. I was, however, only 10 years old at the time. Looking back, I might have been more inclined to stop asking her why if she had given me a genuine explanation about the importance of school and homework in my life, but with six kids in our family, I think she took the most expedient path available to get me to do what she requested.

Students today need more than an "I told you to" reason for learning. Students deserve a clear rationale for why we want them to take on new roles and responsibilities as learners. Without such a rationale, their willingness to buy into a learner-centered environment will be significantly reduced. Telling students the reason they need to do their work is to avoid failure is poor educational practice and does nothing to enlighten them about its value and purpose. This chapter details how we can provide clear and meaningful reasons to students *why* we want them to change their learning practices. It also explains how we can get students to understand that these changes will greatly optimize their learning.

The Rationale for Attending College

Explaining the significant benefits of a college education to our students will help them get excited about and become engaged in learning. The social pressure to attend college is greater now than it has ever been. Students are told that to get a good job and be successful, they must earn a college degree. In other words, a college degree means increased earning potential. Our students need to understand the other important benefits of a college education. They need to know why they are in college beyond "I was told I needed to be here" (DeBard, 2004).

The Benefits of a College Education

Too often, discussions of the benefits of college begin and end with the amount of money a college education is worth. It is said that over a person's lifetime, a college education increases earning potential by $1–$2 million. The economic value of college is certainly not insignificant, but focusing solely on money reinforces the notion that the benefits of a college degree are purely external. We need to balance that perspective by highlighting the other extremely valuable benefits of a college experience, namely, the importance of exploring our internal selves and building lifelong learning skills that will guide us for the rest of our lives.

In "The Value of a College Degree," Porter (2002) identifies the benefits of college beyond money. She cites a 1998 report published by the Institute for Higher Education Policy that identifies the following benefits

- increased personal/professional mobility;
- improved quality of life for their offspring;
- better consumer decision making; and
- more hobbies and leisure activities (pp. 16–17).

Porter also cites reports that the nonmonetary individual benefits of higher education also include the tendency for postsecondary students to become more open-minded, more cultured, more rational, more consistent, and less authoritarian. These benefits are also passed along to succeeding generations (Rowley & Hurtado, 2002).

Additional benefits of college include

- decreased prejudice;
- enhanced knowledge of world affairs;
- enhanced social status; and

- increased economic and job security for those who earn bachelor's degrees.

Porter (2002) also reported that research has consistently shown a positive correlation between completion of college and good health, not only for oneself, but also for one's children, and "increases in schooling levels (and higher relative income) were also found to be positively correlated with lower mortality rates for given age brackets" (Cohn & Geske, 1992).

The Social Value of Higher Education

A number of studies have shown a high correlation between higher education and cultural and family values, and economic growth. According to Cohn and Geske (1992), there is a tendency for more highly educated women to spend more time with their children; these women tend to use this time to better prepare their children for the future. Cohn and Geske also report that college graduates view their future personal progress with greater optimism.

The Public Benefits of Higher Education

In 1998, the Institute for Higher Education Policy reported that the public also benefits when students complete college. These benefits include

- greater tax revenues;
- greater workplace productivity;
- increased consumption;
- increased workforce flexibility; and
- less reliance on government financial support

The conclusion to share with our students is that the benefits of a college degree go far beyond just increased earning potential; they include a better quality of life.

Why Use a Learner-Centered Approach to Teaching

Although it may irritate the teacher, one of the most intelligent questions a student can ask is, "Why do we have to do this?" Students (and the rest of us, for all that) are loathe to expend cognitive energy unnecessarily, so assessing the importance of a task is a key initial step in cognition.

—Robert Sylwester (2003)

One of the most important actions we can take to help our students learn in a learner-centered environment is to continually explain to them why this approach is the best possible way to enhance their learning success. We must illustrate how the knowledge and skills we are asking them to learn are intricately linked to their learning goals, and how the methods we are recommending will enable them to develop learning and thinking skills that will serve them for a lifetime.

The best response we can give our students when they question learner-centered practice is that it incorporates the new discoveries that have been made about how the human brain learns. Our students need to see that we are following the best and latest research as we design our teaching approaches, just as we require them to follow the best research when doing their course work.

Four Rationales for Explaining What and How We Teach

Perhaps nothing is more important in creating a successful learning experience than demonstrating how the knowledge and skills being taught are meaningful to the lives of our students. In the following sections, I provide four rationales that outline, for students, how the teaching methods we choose, and the knowledge and skills we teach, greatly enhance their learning experience.

Teaching in Harmony With the Human Brain

Our desire to incorporate the new discoveries about how the human brain learns informs many of the changes we are introducing. For example, the reason why we want students to do more firsthand learning, group learning, practicing, reflecting, teaching, and presenting is that all of these learning activities require active engagement. We know from neuroscience research that the dendrites of our brain cells grow only when the brain is actively engaged, and that the neuronetworks formed by our brain cells stay connected only when they are put to frequent use (Ratey, 2002, p. 19). We need to continually stress to our students that we are asking them to take on new learning tasks, which require them to adopt new learning roles, to optimize the development of their neuronetworks so they will become successful college learners. (I explore in detail the influence the new research on human learning is having on teaching and learning in chapter 4.)

Preparing Students for Their Careers

The rationale for many of the learning skills, behaviors, attitudes, and critical thinking strategies included in our learner-centered courses is that students will need these skills for their careers. For example, students are put into small groups not just because it promotes a deeper level of learning, but because learning to talk with, or listen to, others is perhaps the single most important skill necessary to be successful in any career. In addition, asking students to make presentations before the whole class enhances the development of speaking skills, which are crucial for career success. Most of the activities we promote and content knowledge we teach has relevance to students' career goals. When students understand that we are preparing them for career success, they are more likely to accept learner-centered teaching.

Preparing Students to Be Lifelong Learners

College is no longer a terminal educational experience, and getting our students to understand this is important. We must replace the idea that, "If we do not teach it to them, then they will never learn it," with "If we do not prepare them to be lifelong learners capable of independent, self-motivated learning, then we have done less than a satisfactory job." One of the reasons students are being asked to take on more responsibility for their own learning is that they will be responsible for it for the rest of their lives. Developing lifelong learning skills is justification for many of the changes students will be asked to make in a learner-centered classroom. We teach lifelong learning skills, such as writing, reading, working well with others, accepting and giving feedback and criticism, expressing ideas clearly and concisely, being on time, listening attentively, defending a position or an idea, and locating reliable information, but we often do not explain *why* we are teaching these skills. Each time we conduct a class activity or give a homework assignment or an assessment, we should point out that these activities are building the lifelong learning skills students will need to compete in an ever-flattening global economy.

Preparing Students for Today, Tomorrow, and Next Semester

The fourth rationale for asking our students to learn new skills and concepts is the one that most of us have been using since we began teaching: they will need it to understand what is presented in their classes tomorrow, next week, or even next semester. This is less a rationale for accepting learner-centered teaching, than it is a universal explanation of why students need to learn the content and skills presented daily in their courses. Helping our students to understand that what they are learning today will be useful and necessary to their future learning creates a powerful reason for them to view all of their learning more seriously. Although we like to think our students can see the relationship between yesterday's lesson and today's, that is not always the case. Telling students how what they are currently being taught will be relevant in their future learning adds purpose to their daily experience.

Painting a More Coherent Picture of What We Ask Students to Learn

One way to help our students engage more fully in learner-centered classrooms is to show them how the skills and knowledge we are asking them to learn are connected to what they are learning in their other courses. Additionally, if we were to give students who are declaring their major not only a checklist of the courses they need to complete, but also a map that illustrates where the skills, major ideas, and concepts learned in their beginning courses (or in their general education courses) will reappear in their later courses, we would be providing clear evidence that their education does not consist of a set of disconnected courses but, rather, an integrated, connected set of skills and knowledge that is purposely designed to prepare them for a lifetime of learning. This map would be a visual representation that learning is not just providing information on a test, but it is developing a coherent set of knowledge and skills that will make students part of the educated citizenry.

This practice is commonplace in K–12 schools, where curricula are mapped to show what knowledge and skills are being taught at each grade level, so parents can see the developmental progress of their child's learning. This is also done so teachers can verify that all of the important skills are being taught and where in the curriculum they appear, and that there are no gaps or overlaps in the content and skills. However, in higher education, mapping is not a common practice, leading students to feel that their education was nothing more than a series of disconnected courses. For example, in *The Learning Paradigm College* (Tagg, 2003), a University of Michigan senior had this to say at the end of his four years of college: "Then comes GRADUATION. And you wake up and you look at this bunch of courses and then it hits you: They don't add up to anything. It's just a bunch of courses. It doesn't mean a thing" (Willimon & Naylor, 1995, pp. 57–58).

Our students need to see that there is a purpose to what they perceive as the unrelated hoops colleges ask them to jump through to graduate. We must provide as much clarity about why they need to learn what is asked of them as we possibly can.

Stakeholders Exercise

Another way to enlighten students about why they need to take on greater responsibility for their learning is through an activity called Stakeholders. A colleague of mine, Dr. Cecil Queen, who teaches in our Criminal Justice Institute, uses Stakeholders each time he introduces a new set of skills or knowledge to his students. The purpose of the exercise is to help students discover reasons beyond a grade for deeply learning the course material presented. In this activity students are asked to identify other people or organizations who are stakeholders in their being successful learners of the new material. Dr. Queen then maps all of the major and minor stakeholders who are depending on his criminal justice students to become fully competent with the new material. Figure 3.1 is a map made when the topic of domestic violence was introduced in his class.

This easy exercise results in students becoming acutely aware that their learning success is not just about them. Students learn that there is a much larger circle of people and organizations depending on them to act responsibly when they make decisions about how much time and effort to put into their learning. At times, lives may even be at stake. Through the Stakeholders exercise, Dr. Queen's students grasp the seriousness of their decisions and see more clearly the tremendous responsibility he has to help them learn. His students come to understand that, with so much at stake, he would never select a teaching approach if he did not believe it was the best and most effective one available.

FIGURE 3.1
Example map for Stakeholders exercise.

Why Students Need Us to Tell Them Why

One of the most important aspects of being a learner-centered teacher is remembering that teaching is, in most ways, no different from any other interaction among humans. If I do not know why you want me to help you with a project, or if I cannot see how taking on a certain task has some benefit to me, I am hesitant to do it. Students' reactions are no different. When we ask students to make significant changes in their roles as learners, it is crucial to explain what's in it for them. Students arrive at college with well-formulated theories about schooling, and about academic institutions in general. These theories are based on their own experiences with school (Tagg, 2003, p. 40). However, these theories don't always include well-thought-out reasons why they are in college and what their expectations are for spending four or five years engaged in the academic, social, and emotional experiences that make up college life. High school students define the payoff of schooling almost exclusively in terms of external rewards (Steinberg, 1996). They believe in the benefits associated with getting a diploma or degree for later success in life, but do not connect this later success with doing well in school or with learning what schools have to teach (Steinberg, 1996, p. 75). If we are to engage our students in active, purposeful learning, it appears that our work is cut out for us. We need to recognize that the content cart cannot be put before the rationale horse. Our students need to understand, first, why what we ask them to learn is important to them and their learning goals, and, second, why the ways in which we ask them to learn—the activities, assignments, and assessments—will optimize their academic success.

An Example of Telling Students Why

Each year the honors program students at Ferris State select one honors faculty member as the outstanding teacher of the year. In 2005, the award was given to my colleague, Dan Adsmond, a chemistry professor. Chemistry is the do-or-die course for acceptance into our pharmacy and optometry professional doctorate programs, so the mere fact that the students picked a chemistry professor tells you that Dan must be doing something special. A grade of less than an A does not endear a professor to his students. Dan does not give away As, so when he was asked at the awards ceremony why he felt the students chose him as the outstanding teacher of the year, he credited it to a lesson on the importance of creating relevance for students' learning. Dan said he always explains *why* to his students. Whether it is why he wants them to learn a certain aspect of chemistry or why he wants them to use a certain learning tool, he feels his students deserve to know the rationale for his request. Dan also said he believes that, once his students understand his reasons, they become more willing to engage in, and work hard at, their learning. The simple act of explaining to his students why he wanted them to learn certain content and skills is why Dan won the award.

The Power of Telling Students Why

Part of the power of creating relevance lies in the control it gives students over their own learning. The need for control among learners is so powerful that no outside influence or force can cause the brain to learn. It must decide on its own (Zull, 2002). If we want our students to learn, we must help them feel in control (p. 52). If people believe something is important to their lives, they will learn it. If we want people to learn, we must help them see how their learning matters (p. 52). We must tell them *why*.

When students do not understand why certain learning is important or how it will help them reach their goals, they are left with few clear reasons to put effort into their learning beyond getting a grade and checking one more course off their graduation checklist. The faculty complaint I hear most often is that students do not seem to care about learning. Learners of all ages are more motivated when they can see the usefulness of what they are learning, and when they can use that information to do something that has an impact on others—especially their local community (McCombs, 1996; Pintrich & Schunk, 1996). If we are to help our students understand why the learning we are asking them to do is relevant to their schooling, their lives, and their futures, we must build a case for this relevance. In the following sections, I give examples of rationales for five different aspects of teaching and learning: lecturing, using reflective journals, asking students to make classroom presentations, using cumulative testing, and discussing assigned readings. These rationales represent the kind of information we need to share with students if we are to make learning more meaningful for them.

Lecturing

At a recent meeting I attended with a group of nursing faculty to discuss their plans to adopt a learner-centered approach in the courses required for their new BSN degree, one of them let out a heavy sigh of relief when I said that lecturing certainly played an important role in a learner-centered classroom. I was left with the distinct impression that she was not alone in her belief that somehow learner-centered practice means no lecture. That belief could not be further from the truth. The purpose of lecturing is to explain ideas and concepts that students cannot easily learn on their own. No one is better suited to explain the difficult, challenging, and complex information that is a part of all college courses than an expert teacher. A teacher with years of experience in the subject area—an individual who can provide many great analogies, metaphors, and examples, and knows how to use these teaching tools to connect the challenging material to his or her students' background knowledge, clearly should be the one doing most of the talking. This process has been a vital part of the learning process in higher education for centuries. It is only when lectures waste students' time by including information they can learn better on their own, depriving them of learning from their peers through discussion, or causing them to stop reading their textbook because everything in it will be discussed in the lecture, that lecturing becomes a poor choice of teaching methodology.

Taking the time to explain to students why you will be lecturing on some days (because for certain material it is the best way to optimize their learning) and not on others is a big step in helping them to adjust to the new roles and responsibilities they will face in a learner-centered classroom. Many students with whom I interact on my campus see lecture and teaching as synonymous. By helping students to realize that our job includes much more than just telling them information and asking them to repeat it back to us, we are setting the stage for improved student learning. Lecturing plays a vital role in the college experience. However, to determine the best use of lecture in our courses, we must ask ourselves each time we plan a daily lesson, "Is telling my students this information the optimal way for them to learn this material?"

Using Reflective Journals

A weekly reflective journal is a powerful tool for deepening learning and promoting long-term recall of information. Students can be asked to reflect on how the previous week's learning changed their thinking about a topic, how it improved their understanding of previously learned material, or how it altered their view of themselves or the world. However, when students receive this assignment without a clear rationale for doing it, many of them will see it as busywork. Furthermore, many students will spend only a few moments of thought on what they learned and how it changed their thinking and write the first thing that comes to mind. Their entire journal entry may be only two to three sentences unless the teacher has assigned a required numbers of words to be written. However, if students are given the "why" behind reflective journal writing and how it helps their learning, the resulting journal entries are likely to be much more substantive.

The rationale for assigning a reflective journal is to get students to make connections between the new course information and their previous knowledge. These connections are strengthened and expanded when students write about this new information, what it means, and how it can be used. These expanded connections increase the likelihood that this new information will be remembered, as it is now connected to multiple memories, not just one. Some of these connections may trigger emotional responses, as students think about how the new information affects their lives or futures. Emotional connections create an even greater opportunity for recall because emotional pathways are the strongest for creating memory recall (Sprenger, 1999, p. 75).

Reflective journaling greatly enhances students' understanding and recall because the very act of writing causes them to move their ideas from the abstract world inside their brains into the concrete world outside their brains. Writing causes them to translate this new learning into their own words and produce it in a clear and organized manner, which will only be possible if they understand what they've learned. This transference of information signals the student and the teacher about whether the material has been comprehended, providing important assessment information.

Another benefit of journaling is that students engage with the information through touch and movement (tactile and kinesthetic processes), which offers the opportunity to encode the information through additional sensory patterns, thus aiding their retrieval ability.

Finally, reflection, which is one of the main components of reflective journaling, is necessary for humans to fully connect new information to the patterns of knowledge they already possess (Zull, 2002, p. 17). Reflection is one of the most important learning processes we can use.

Figure 3.2 provides a list of rationales for using reflective journals as a learning enhancement tool. These reasons will help students to understand the many values of journaling.

Making Classroom Presentations

The dreaded assignment to speak in front of others has long been the least favorite assignment for college students. The ability to speak in front of others, however, is one of the most important skills students need to learn to be successful professionally. According to William Hewlett, cofounder of Hewlett-Packard, "The ability to clearly communicate ideas to clients and colleagues is a rare skill, yet one that often makes the difference in whether or not a great concept succeeds."

There are several rationales for having students make classroom presentations, one of the most effective learning strategies available to teachers. Presentations help students to develop creativity; critical thinking, technology, writing, speaking, and research skills; professional behaviors such as self-introduction and acknowledgment of others; and the ability to deal with

FIGURE 3.2
Why students should do reflective journaling.

1. It maximizes the opportunity for students to understand new material by expanding the connections to previously learned material.
2. It expands students' current views of the world by helping them to see how the new material might alter their current view of the world or of themselves.
3. It increases the number of neuronetwork connections, increasing the likelihood that students will be able to recall the information in the future.
4. It expands the number of cues that students can respond to in order to recall the new information.
5. It increases the number of neuronetworks for the new learning by coding it through the tactile and kinesthetic senses.
6. It follows the natural way the brain processes information.
7. It helps students to make emotional connections with the new information, enhancing ease of recall.
8. It helps students to move from being receivers of knowledge to producers of knowledge.

criticism, to name just a few. To help students better understand why presentations expand their learning, I have developed a list of 16 learning benefits that result from this activity, which are listed in figure 3.3. Each represents a rationale for explaining to students why we want them to do presentations as a way of expanding their learning.

Cumulative Testing

During every presentation I make, I tell faculty that if they do not change anything else in their teaching as a result of the presentation, they should start giving cumulative tests and exams. I tell them that this one change, for the limited amount of effort it will take, will likely produce more improved student learning than any other change they could make using the same amount of effort. I also remind faculty that the definition of learning is students still having the ability to use what they have learned, even after significant periods of disuse (Bjork, 1994, p. 187). It is my hope that faculty will see that cumulative testing causes students to relearn, review, and practice key information and skills a great deal more than do traditional forms of testing. By requiring students to practice and review throughout the semester, faculty are using a highly effective way for students to form the long-term memories that represent real learning (Ratey, 2002, p. 191).

FIGURE 3.3
Rationales for giving presentations.

1. Students will need to deeply learn the information to be presented. If people are going to inform others about what they know, they must first understand the material fully themselves.
2. Students will learn to organize information in a clear and concise way. The audience is interested in hearing the most important information. Students must be prepared to give it to them.
3. Students will learn to use analysis skills to find the most important information to share. Their research needs to lead them to the most important and interesting ideas. These are what the audience wants to hear.
4. Students will learn to think about the audience—who these individuals are and how best to connect with them.
5. Students will learn to use visual aids to enhance their ideas. By their very nature, people are visual (Zull, 2002, p. 144). The proper use of images can greatly enhance the message of the presentation.
6. Students will learn where to find effective visual images to enhance their presentation. There is a whole world beyond their computer's clip art. There are computer graphics, digitized photographic stills, photo mosaics, geographic information systems, video simulations, and visualizations that apply three- and four-dimensional computer graphics technologies.
7. Students will learn to use presentation tools such as PowerPoint and Internet sites.
8. Students will learn how to practice their presentation to enhance their presenting skills. The act of practicing can make giving their presentation easier. Students will learn how to fit information into a set time period.
9. Students will learn how to relax in front of an audience.
10. Students will learn how to help their peers to learn. They will discover what it takes to teach others.
11. Students will learn how to accept feedback on their presentation and use it to improve future presentations.
12. Students will learn that most professional jobs require presentation skills.
13. Students will learn that if they cannot explain a topic to others, then it is very likely that they do not clearly understand the topic themselves.
14. Students will learn to do research on the topic and discover new sources of information in their field of study.
15. Students will learn to defend their views in front of others. This extremely important real-world skill will be vital to their professional success.
16. Students will learn to build a case with evidence to prove a point or defend a position.

The rationale for using cumulative exams is that they force students to review and relearn much of their course material by continually retesting the important information that was to be learned in each section of the course. In addition, cumulative testing helps students to see the connections between the information they learned in the first part of the course and the material that comes later.

In the summer of 2006, I completed a study of the differences in the number of interactions students have with their course material (interactions that are key to forming long-term memories) in a typical teacher-centered class with no cumulative exams, and in a learner-centered class with cumulative exams. I found that the learner-centered students had many more interactions with course material in just the first four weeks of the course than did students in the teacher-centered course had over the entire 16 weeks of the semester. Part of the large discrepancy between the two groups was the result of the learner-centered teacher using additional learning activities to enhance the interactions students had with the material, in addition to giving cumulative exams.

The study revealed that many students in the teacher-centered course limited their interactions with the course material to listening to the lecture, recording the information into notes, reading about the information in the textbook, and then, four weeks later, studying for an extended period of time (cramming) the night before the test. These students interacted with the material only 4 or 5 times over a 4-week period, with most of the interaction occurring on the day the material was introduced in class and the day before it was tested. This limited interaction made it more difficult to form long-lasting memories of the material. Figure 3.4 shows the dramatic difference in the number of opportunities the learner-centered and the teacher-centered students were given with the course material during the first 4 weeks of the semester.

Researchers who study memory have made it clear that cramming before an exam involves the working memory and does not significantly aid in the creation of long-term memories (Zull, 2002, p. 181). Students can indeed hold the information crammed into their working memories for extended periods of time—periods long enough to get an A on an exam—without that information becoming a part of their long-term memory (p. 181). I call the kind of teaching that allows students to pass a test but form few long-term

FIGURE 3.4
**Differences in number of learning opportunities during the
first four weeks of the semester.**

	Cram-Centered	Learner-Centered
Pre-class reading assignment	☑	☑
Brainstorming	☐	☑
Lecture	☑	☑
Note taking	☑	☑
Breakout to discuss first part of lecture	☐	☑
End of lecture formative assignment	☐	☑
Make concept map of notes	☐	☑
Review notes	☐	☑
At least 3 times a week study for weekly quiz	☐	☑
Weekly quiz	☐	☑
Reflective Journal	☐	☑
Test review	☑	☑
Study for test 2–3 days before	☐	☑
Study day before test	☑	☑
Test	☑	☑

memories cram-centered teaching. My informal study shows that learner-centered teachers choose learning and assessment activities that promote long-term memory formation. These activities cause those students who do the activities to practice, in various ways, the knowledge and skills to be learned many times, thereby optimizing their opportunities to form long-term memories.

Discussing Assigned Readings

When I take the time to explain to my students why we will spend a great deal of time discussing the readings assigned in my courses, the payoffs are significant. I tell my students that there are several rationales for using classroom discussion as a learning tool, but the most important benefit is the development of their speaking and listening skills. I explain that they will spend more time using speaking and listening skills in their careers and personal lives than any other skill set they will learn in college. I point out that their career success may depend on their ability to express their ideas clearly, quickly, and in an organized fashion and to focus on the most important information so others can understand it easily. I stress that the ability to listen attentively to what others are saying and be able to respond intelligently to their ideas and questions is vital to their success, not only in the workplace but in their personal lives as well. I also discuss the deep learning that comes from discussion and how valuable it is to the development of their thinking abilities to see how others think and perceive the ideas and viewpoints in the assigned readings.

If we want our students to engage fully in classroom discussion, we need to help them see how necessary it is to their future success. In chapter 6, I explore the skills that our students need to be effective at talking and listening.

A Final Thought

Those of us who make our living in higher education probably learned a great many things as undergraduates without clearly knowing the rationale behind why we were being asked to learn them. We survived without this knowledge because most of us loved learning and were highly motivated to succeed. However, most of us would have found the learning more enjoyable, useful, and valuable had we understood *why* we were being asked to learn the content (Bransford et al., 2000, p. 5). With two-thirds of high school graduates now starting college within 2 years of high school graduation (Carey, 2005, p. 1), and with the demographics profile changing significantly since the 1990s, students today, more than ever before, need clear "whys" and "hows" if they are to succeed; telling them, "because I said so," just won't cut it.

4

PUTTING STUDENTS' LEARNING INTO THE CONTEXT OF CURRENT LEARNING THEORY

All our knowledge has its origins in our perceptions.

—Leonardo da Vinci

How People Learn (Bransford et al., 2000), an accounting of the research findings from the past 20 years that have contributed most powerfully to our understanding of human learning and teaching, makes the following conclusions about teacher preparedness:

- Teachers need to develop an understanding of the theories of knowledge (epistemologies) that guide the subject-matter disciplines in which they work.
- Teachers need a knowledge base (an epistemology) of pedagogy, including knowledge of how cultural beliefs and the personal characteristics of learners influence learning.

In other words, if we are to optimize our students' learning, we need to have a reasonable understanding of how our students learn and the factors that affect their learning. This chapter is about providing that understanding. Without knowledge of epistemologies and pedagogy, we cannot possibly create meaningful rationales for our students to learn the knowledge and skills we ask them to learn, nor can we expect them to participate in the many learning activities that facilitate their learning.

In chapter 3, the first suggestion I offered for creating relevance for learner-centered teaching was to place the learning activities in the context of the current understanding of how humans learn. Of all the existing research about how the human brain learns, and all the evidence provided by cognitive psychologists, this chapter focuses on five major findings. These findings are key to explaining to students why the new roles and responsibilities that we ask students to take on in a learner-centered classroom will optimize their learning. These findings can also guide us as we examine our teaching practice. This examination process is vital to the well-being of our students. Just as a doctor must reexamine patient care when medical science discovers new drug treatments and therapies, we must reexamine the way we teach when new research about human learning becomes available. For us to do otherwise would be irresponsible.

Talking With Students About How Humans Learn

Faculty ask me regularly to talk with their students about brain research and learning. The faculty who invite me to speak are usually expecting two results. The first is to get their students to better understand that the course assignments, tests, and other course learning activities they are using are in harmony with our understanding of how people learn. The second is to get their students to see that activities such as daily review, study partners, concept mapping, and reflection activities, such as journaling, are powerful tools in the creation of long-lasting learning.

These undergraduate students, even those who are premed and prepharmacy, often have very little understanding of how their brains work with regard to learning. They are unaware of *why* certain assignments and course activities are the most effective tools in the formation of the long-term memories they need to be successful college students and lifelong learners. When I discuss the discoveries neuroscientists have made about how humans learn, the students appear interested, but, more important, they seem to understand why their teachers are asking them to engage in certain classroom practices. Understanding the latest research about how the brain learns makes their own learning process more relevant.

The five areas of learning research that are the focus of this chapter are:

1. Neurons and neuronetworks
2. Patterns in new information

3. The role of learning activities in promoting long-term recall
4. The effect of fear and stress
5. The power of images

For a more in-depth look at current research and theories about teaching and learning, see Bransford et al., 2000; Caine and Caine, 1997; Goldberg, 2002; Ratey, 2002; Sylwester, 1995; Zull, 2002.

Neurons and Neuronetworks

Ask your students this question: "How many of you know the lyrics to songs you didn't even try to learn or, even stranger, didn't even want to learn?" Many of your students will say they do. Just about all of us have lyrics floating around in our heads. Many say that not only do they have these songs in their head, but they "play" at some of the oddest times. How do we learn these lyrics without any conscious effort on our part? The neuronetworks in the brain that represent the lyrics were fired repeatedly each time the songs were heard. The more often lyrics are heard or sung, the stronger the neuronetworks for these songs become, until the lyrics and music become long-term memories. Learning songs is a simple example of how long-term memory formation takes place. If the new information is used enough, the neuronetworks for that information become strong and long-lasting (Ratey, 2002, p. 5). The opposite is equally true. For example, if our students do not use the information learned in their courses, the neuronetworks for that information will not remain in place, and no long-term memories will be formed (p. 5).

As students continually use new information, the neuronetworks for this new information fire again and again, thus increasing the likelihood that the neuronetworks will remain bound together. The faster a neuron fires (each time a neuronetwork for new learning is fired, the speed at which it can fire in the future is increased), the greater the electrical charge it generates and the more likely it is to set off its neighboring neurons. This process is called long-term potentiation (LTP). The result is that the repeated firing (e.g., as occurs in engaging in daily review) binds the neurons together, so if one fires they all fire, ultimately forming a memory trace. These traces allow new learning to associate and form networks with similar information that already exists, thereby making this larger, consolidated memory easier to retrieve (Sousa, 2001, p. 80).

It is possible, however, to form long-lasting memories without this repeated firing of neuronetworks. For example, when a learner has a strong emotional experience, he or she can remember these experiences more easily, and they endure better over time (Ratey, 2002, p. 209). For most course learning, though, following the rule, "use it or lose it," is the key (Sprenger, 1999, p. 23).

Learning Is an Ongoing Process

To build a strong rationale for the use of quizzing, lecture summaries, homework problems, daily review sessions, recitations, class discussions, and reflection journals, we need to constantly remind our students that all of these activities fire and wire their neurons, enabling them to form long-term memories. Our students need to understand that long-term memory formation takes time and continual engagement with course material. They need to understand that studying once every three or four weeks is not enough to learn the lecture material.

There is additional research about how the brain stores and uses information that goes hand-in-hand with the firing and wiring of neurons: each time a person retrieves something from long-term memory and moves it into working memory, he or she relearns it (Sousa, 2001, p. 107). The significance of this finding is the rationale it provides for frequent quizzing, recitation, small- and large-group discussion, and many other commonly used learning activities that require students to recall what they have already learned. This relearning process deepens learning and helps to create long-term memories for the particular information or skill.

Patterns in New Information

> Experts notice features and meaningful patterns of information that are not noticed by novices.
>
> —Bransford et al., 2000, p. 31.

In his book, *A User's Guide to the Brain*, Dr. James Ratey (2002) describes the brain as a pattern-seeking device: "The brain is an analog processor, meaning, essentially, that it works by analogy and metaphor. It relates whole concepts to one another and looks for similarities, differences, and relationships between them" (p. 5). The ability to recognize the patterns that exist in various subjects and use them to solve problems, even problems outside the subject area, is what separates experienced learners and experts from novice learners. The notion that experts recognize features and patterns that novices do not is potentially very important for improving instruction (e.g., Bransford, Sherwood, & Hasselbring, 1988; Sabers, Cushing, & Berliner, 1991).

Students come to higher education possessing a range of knowledge, skills, beliefs, and concepts that significantly influences what they notice about the environment and how they organize and interpret it. This, in turn, affects their abilities to remember, reason, solve problems, and acquire new knowledge (Bransford et al., 1988). Most undergraduates are novice learners. Their ability to recognize the patterns within the subjects we teach is limited by their background knowledge and the kinds of educational training they received before entering college. One of the most important things we can do as teachers is to show our students how to look for and use the patterns of information in our subjects. Experiments with chess masters have shown that what separates the masters from the novices, and even from the good players, is their incredible ability to see the possible patterns of movement in any given game situation.

Research has shown that, when viewing instructional texts, slides, and videotapes, for example, the information novices notice can be quite different from what experts notice. One dimension of acquiring greater competence appears to be the greater ability to segment the perceptual field or learn how to see. Research on expertise suggests the importance of providing students with learning experiences that specifically enhance their ability to recognize meaningful patterns of information (e.g., Bransford, Franks, Vye, & Sherwood, 1989; Simon, 1980).

When we ask our students to compare and contrast, to find similarities and differences, to build timelines, to put things in an outline, to create concept maps, to find the main ideas and significant details, we are asking them to engage in tasks that use familiar patterns. When new information is introduced to students, one of the first actions of their brain is to determine whether the information is novel or already exists in their memory banks as a familiar pattern. The brain looks for patterns of similarity to other previously learned material as a way of knowing what to connect the new information to and what appropriate actions to take. It is when the brain cannot find a similar pattern that we may have a look of confusion on our face and momentarily feel like we are back in kindergarten.

The following two-step exercise demonstrates the brain's desire to look for patterns, and how much easier information is to learn when it fits into a familiar pattern. This exercise will help students understand the importance of finding patterns in the material they are asked to learn.

1. Read the following numbers and try to memorize them in the exact order in which they are listed:

     5807652972

     This is not an overly difficult task, but it would take some time and repetition to remember all of the numbers in sequence, because the numbers as separate, unrelated items would exceed the capacity of our working memory.

2. Look at the numbers again with a pattern imposed on them:

     (580) 765–2927
     OR
     5,807,652,972

     Each of these familiar patterns makes the task of recalling the numbers easier for two reasons: first, the patterns are familiar to us; we have used them many times, and, second, the patterns add meaning to the numbers. The numbers go from being an unrelated list of digits to a meaningful phone number or the budget of a small country. The addition of the pattern allows the working memory to see the numbers as chunks of information, which now easily fit within the capacity of the working memory

Patterns exist within all of our subjects. Helping students to see the patterns imbedded in your particular content is of great importance in optimizing their learning opportunities. Different domains of knowledge, such as science, mathematics, and history, have different organizing properties. It follows, therefore, that having an in-depth grasp of an area requires knowledge about both the content of the subject and the broader structural organization of the subject (Bransford et al., 2000, p. 36).

Many students are used to seeing information presented in a very linear format and may have some difficulty recognizing patterns that are nonlinear, such as in the social sciences, where information is often organized around big ideas (Voss, Greene, Post, & Penner, 1983). The pattern for subjects that have a central concept or pivotal idea, and information builds on this idea with varying degrees of importance depending on the context or circumstances of the learning, will be less familiar to most undergraduates.

The fact that experts have organized their knowledge around important ideas or concepts suggests that curricula should also be organized in ways that lead to conceptual understanding. Many approaches to curriculum design make it difficult for students to organize knowledge meaningfully. Often there is only superficial coverage of facts before moving on to the next topic; there is little time to develop important, organizing ideas (Bransford et al., 2000, p. 42).

Effective comprehension and thinking require a coherent understanding of the organizing principles in any subject matter. Understanding the essential features of the problems of various school subjects will lead to better reasoning and problem solving (Bransford et al., 2000, p. 42). The notion of helping students organize their knowledge also suggests that novices might benefit from models of how experts approach problem solving—especially if they then receive coaching in using similar strategies (e.g., Brown, Collins, & Duguid, 1989).

Teachers have forever been asking students to make outlines, draw concept maps, and find similarities and differences between the ideas in one book and those found in another. By helping students understand the brain's desire to find and use patterns of information, we are creating a rationale for many of the assignments we give them. Finding and using patterns that will allow students to understand the concepts and ideas they are learning more deeply can improve their ability to transfer the information from one context to another. Like the chess master, they will have many possible moves available to them when problems arise.

The Role of Learning Activities in Promoting Long-Term Recall

One of the primary functions of the front integrative cortex of the brain is working memory. This part of the brain helps us recall information we encountered seconds, minutes, and sometimes hours ago (Zull, 2002, p. 180). It would be easy for students to think that the information they are reviewing the night before a test will go from their working memory into their long-term memory. The fact is, working memory and long-term memory involve separate pathways in the brain (p. 181). Because it is possible for students to hold quite a bit of information in their working memories long enough to pass an exam (cramming), they believe that they learned this information, especially if they received a high grade. However, as we all know, if you ask students who crammed to share their learning a week or two after an exam, they will be hard-pressed to come up with all or even part of it. They are unable to retrieve the information because it never made its way into long-term memory.

It is not that working memory is unrelated to long-term memory; clearly, information that starts in working memory often becomes part of long-term memory if it is used enough. Getting students to use the information enough is where we come into play. We must design the kinds of learning activities and assessments that promote long-term memory formation. Additionally, we need to make it clear to our students that cramming for a test is a hollow victory. As I mentioned in chapter 3, the rationale for giving a cumulative exam is that it causes students to relearn and review course material enough times for the information to become stored in their long-term memory, where it can really do them some good.

The Effect of Fear and Stress

Why is developing a classroom community where learners feel safe and trust exists between the teacher and the learners so important? Why is creating an environment where learners have some say in their learning and can exhibit some control over what happens to them vital to a learner-centered practice? Studies that explore the effects of attitudes and emotions on learning indicate that prolonged stress and fear, at any age, can circumvent the brain's normal learning process (Sylwester, 1995). A person's physical and emotional well-being is closely linked to his or her ability to think and learn effectively. Emotionally stressful home or school environments are counterproductive to learning. Although teachers cannot control all influences on a young person's sense of safety and well-being, they can build an atmosphere of trust and intellectual safety that will optimize students' opportunities to learn (p. 22).

At its very essence, the human brain is interested in only one thing—staying alive. Therefore, it is important for us as teachers to understand to what extent the brain will go to protect itself. Zull (2002) refers to the amygdala, a small almond-shaped cluster of cells, as the "fear region of the brain" (p. 57). Although the amygdala plays a role in other emotions as well, fear and the related emotions of anger and rage seem to originate primarily in this region (p. 57). When students are feeling fear, anxiety, or stress, they become focused on these emotions, not on learning.

A very real issue for us as teachers is that stress and fear can highjack our students' attention and, as a result, inhibit learning (Goldman, 1996). If the stress and fear originate from life issues that are clearly beyond our control, there is little we can do. However, if we are the cause of these feelings, then it is up to us to change our behaviors and classroom environments to help our students feel safer and more at ease. If our students are experiencing fear and stress, which means their amygdalas are active, then the kind of active learning we are asking them to engage in will likely be negatively affected. How much stress or fear must be present to affect students' learning is difficult to predict. What is known is that classroom environments that give students some say about their learning, thus giving them a sense of control over the learning process, have a positive effect on learning (Zull, 2002, p. 60).

For all of the amazing things that the human brain can do, it can pay attention to only one thing at a time (Marois, 2005). If students are fearful or anxious because of the classroom environment or their relationship with the teacher or other students, their attention is quite likely to be focused on that fear or anxiety, not on learning. I am not suggesting that teachers and learning environments should not be challenging, or that expectations for students' learning should not be high. Nor am I suggesting that students should not be placed in authentic stressful environments as a way of developing the skills they will need to be successful in those environments as graduates. My point is that if we do not recognize that learning is negatively affected by environments that are not conducive to social and emotional trust and safety, then we are far from optimizing our students' learning.

One powerful way to reduce students' stress is to provide them with more ownership of their learning. We need to give students choices about issues surrounding their learning, including policies about course attendance, tardiness to class, late assignments, and makeup tests; classroom behavior issues; forms of assessment used; due dates of assignments; writing or research topics (when appropriate); and discussion guidelines. These choices will give students a greater feeling of control over their learning situation, allowing them to engage more fully because they have ownership of the process. When students have a say in course decisions, they also take on more responsibility for complying with those decisions. For example, when students decide what the attendance policy will be, and someone in the class violates that policy, it is up to the students, the community of learners, of which the violator is a member, to enforce the rule, not the teacher. It is difficult to argue with a rule you helped to create. Actions that give students choices and more control over their learning help the learning process shift subtly from the teacher always being in charge and making the learning decisions to the community of learners working together to find the best ways for them to learn. This creates an environment that can help keep fear and stress in check. An additional benefit of students being given learning choices is that they have greater interest in the topic to be researched or discussed. It is simple human nature to put more effort into those things we care about, or are interested in, than those that are dictated to us.

Students do not always embrace the concept of making choices and taking more control of their learning, at least not right away. As I discussed in chapter 2, students have strong beliefs about what school is supposed to be, and having a lot of choices is not one of them. Helping students see the personal growth that can result from making learning choices and accepting responsibility for them is a key element of a learner-centered practice. We may need to introduce choices and control gradually, however, to get students to accept this concept.

The Power of Images

Different features of learning contribute to the durability or fragility of memory. For example, comparisons of people's memories for words with their memories for pictures of the same objects show that pictures are far superior for memory recall. This effect is also true when words and pictures are combined during learning (Roediger, 1997). This finding has direct relevance for improving long-term learning of certain kinds of information. In studies done on the macaque monkey's visual system, which is one of the most understood and best models we have for human vision to date, researchers found that 50% of the sensory cortex of the macaque was made up of the visual cortex (Schmolesky, 1998). Likewise, humans are very visual learners. The brain's ability to visualize is arguably the most significant aspect of cognition in humans (Zull, 2002, p. 138).

The visual world is literally and physically mapped on our brain (Zull, 2002, p. 144). What we see in the world is more than just the concrete object we are looking at; it is also a whole set of conceptual relationships for the object. When we look at a house, we do not just see a house; the networks firing in our brain may cause us to think about the cost of the house, how the house compares to our home, or perhaps even to feel jealousy. Every memory we have comes to us as an image. As teachers, we need to recognize that images are the easiest things for the brain to remember (p. 145).

For many years I taught a first-year seminar course, one topic of which was basic nutrition. I knew I could talk until I was exhausted about the need to eat right and reduce fat and sugar intake and still have little or no impact on my students. So I decided to create powerful images of the fat and sugar found in the common foods and drinks my students consumed. I brought to class a 20-ounce bottle of cola, a sugar bowl, a teaspoon, and a clear glass. I asked the students to tell me to stop when they thought I had put the same amount of sugar that was in the soda into the glass. Needless to say, my students told me to stop many times before I reached the real stopping point of 13 teaspoons of sugar. I held up the glass, which was almost 30% full, and asked if anyone would like to eat the sugar. The image of the glass was so powerful that nearly every student's course evaluation said it was one of the most effective methods I had used to teach them. I repeated this process for the fat in a Whopper and a Big Mac using a stick of butter. Again, the image is what made them remember the importance of eating right.

When we want our students to demonstrate their understanding of the concepts and ideas we teach, we often ask them to translate these more abstract ideas into concrete images by giving examples, by showing how something works or how it could be applied. The reason why we ask our students to illustrate their findings or draw a concept map, or why we take them on field trips, is that the images they see and the connections they form make it easier to remember what they are learning. This is also why we use pictures and images in lectures and demonstrations.

Explaining to Students That Research Drove the Change to Learner-Centered Teaching

By explaining to our students that we adopted a learner-centered approach to teaching because the research indicates that it is the best possible way to improve students' learning, we create a powerful rationale for its use. A great example of how this research guides educational practice can be found in the approach taken by the nursing faculty at Ferris State. Our nursing faculty tell their students that, when they become practicing nurses, they must let the research inform their practice. When better procedures for patient care are developed, they must be implemented. So, when the nursing program decided to develop a new BSN degree, it let the research on teaching and learning inform its practice and put in place a learner-centered teaching approach that each faculty member has agreed to implement. The nursing faculty simply chose not to ignore the new research findings. I suggest we make the same argument to our students. As new research findings about human learning became known, we had no choice but to change our approach from teacher-centered to learner-centered. Our students need to understand that we have an obligation to incorporate the research on teaching and learning into our practice, and that includes implementing new roles and responsibilities for them as learners. For example, knowing what I do about the limited learning value of cramming for tests, I cannot continue to give tests that can easily be "crammed for." I have to move to cumulative exams. We need to create learning activities and assessments that are in harmony with research findings about the best ways to help students learn. The research must inform the practice.

5

PROMOTING INDEPENDENT LEARNING

If teachers are to prepare an ever more diverse
group of students for much more challenging
work—for framing problems; finding, integrating
and synthesizing information; creating new solutions; learning on their own; and working coop-
eratively—they will need substantially more
knowledge and radically different skills than
most now have and most schools of education
now develop.
      —Darling-Hammond, 1997, p. 154

One of the basic facts all teachers know about the learning process
is that the one who does the work does the learning. As learner-
centered teachers, we must increase the opportunities for students
to learn on their own, and we must develop activities that let them do the
work.

Two factors must be kept in mind as we involve our students in more
independent work. First, many of our students have not been prepared to do
a great deal of learning on their own. Second, it is our responsibility to teach
them the skills necessary to do this. These independent learning skills
(adapted from work done at the University of Surrey, University Skills Program), outlined below, include the ability to handle four areas of task
management:

1. Task analysis is the ability to analyze an assignment and determine
   what needs to be done. This includes drawing up a timeline for completion, breaking the task down into manageable parts, establishing

goals and a framework, identifying an audience that needs the information/findings, and recognizing similarities to previous assignments.

2. Identifying resources and planning actions involves two skill areas. The first is the ability to identify the resources available to assist in completing the task, including the learner's own self-knowledge and skills. The second is developing a plan of action for completing the task based on the resources that have been identified.

3. Taking action based on planning consists of bringing together all of the identified resources and executing the plan that has been developed. A variety of strategies should be used to meet the learning task goals, and the process should be continuously monitored and modified by the student, updating the plan as necessary to reach the final goal.

4. Assessing actions and revising plans takes place after the task has been completed. At that time the student should review the outcome and the effectiveness of the actions taken. Reviewing includes reflecting on the entire process to determine what a student might have learned about himself or herself and his or her learning practice as well as analyzing feedback from others with an eye to improving future work. (University of Surrey, University Skills Program, 2006)

These four areas of independent task management, which play an important role in independent work models, are vital for students to be successful in learner-centered environments. However, they also represent valuable learning skills that will serve students well for the rest of their lives. This chapter outlines strategies for teaching students the skills they need to manage learning tasks independently. It also explains why these skills are best taught as an integrated part of the course subject matter.

Rationales for Learning on One's Own

When we ask students to solve a problem, deal with a case study, or do research on their own, we are engaging them in firsthand learning. Firsthand learning activities require students to transfer information learned in the classroom, or gained from their own life experiences, to the task assigned. This process teaches them to think independently and trust their own analytical abilities. It also helps them learn how to evaluate and engage with sources, whether books, articles, search engines, or human resources, to determine their usefulness for the task at hand. Learning to evaluate sources, a key element in firsthand learning, is one of the most important lifelong learning skills students can develop. The ability to find and organize the right information to solve a problem leads to a deep understanding of the problem-solving process, which leads, in turn, to a greater ability to solve problems independently and with confidence.

When students have the ability to learn on their own, they will know how to generate questions and how to tell the difference between information that will help them complete a task and information that will not. They will know how to identify resources and methods of investigation and how to organize their findings and effectively communicate their results. But perhaps the most valuable outcome is the satisfaction they will experience when they are responsible for their own success. When students prove to themselves that they can be independent learners, capable of thinking for themselves and figuring out how to find and use knowledge in meaningful ways to solve real-world problems, their confidence will grow dramatically. Their accomplishments will bring a feeling of empowerment that will drive their ability to learn for the rest of their lives.

But what if they fail? Failure is painful, but it can also be transformed into a meaningful learning experience. When students discover what they did wrong and figure out how to do better the next time, they are gaining a powerful lifelong learning skill. Failure can actually be a great teacher, if students are taught how to learn from it. UCLA psychologist Robert Bjork (1994) suggests that a vital question for effective learning is, where do we want our students to make their mistakes? The answer, of course, is with us, in our classrooms, where we can help them turn failure into a new opportunity to learn.

Where Should Students Learn to Become Independent Learners?

The best place to teach students how to learn on their own is in our content courses. Such courses represent authentic learning environments where independent learning skills can be developed and practiced with meaningful learning tasks. In addition, the motivation for students to develop better independent learning skills is much greater in environments where grades are given.

Most faculty hired between 1970 and 1995 probably were hired with the understanding that their most important, and often only, teaching responsibility was to teach their content. Whether students were ready to learn the content was not a faculty concern. If anyone had a concern about students' readiness to learn, it was the admissions office. If students needed to learn how to study, how to learn a subject area, or how to learn on their own, they were told to take a study or learning skills course or a course in how to be successful in college. The problem with this approach was that students who enrolled in these kinds of courses were engaged in what psychologists call *far transfer activities*, meaning that the skills being taught were only distantly related to the subject matter in which they were to be used. Transferring these skills from a learning skills course to a subject matter course is not an easy process (Hattie, Biggs, & Purdie, 1996). However, when these learning skills were taught as part of the content course—*near transfer*—the results were always impressive. It is much easier for students to apply study/learning skills productively when they are included in a subject matter course. For example, the best place to learn how to take notes in a history class is in a history class (Huang, 1992)!

Hattie and colleagues (1996) found success in near transfer across a wide range of studies, but considerably less success with far transfer. The findings of White and Frederiksen (1998), which state that the best place to teach metacognitive skills (skills that are crucial to independent learning) is in the subject matter the students are learning, confirm the earlier findings. They found that teaching learning skills in context improved performance in a variety of subject areas.

The best place for students to develop independent learning and college success skills is in the environment where they will put these skills to use, or at least in an environment in which the skills have a direct connection (near transfer) to the course. Programs that have been successful in teaching learning skills outside content courses include Supplemental Instruction developed at the University of Missouri at Kansas City and Structured Learning Assistance developed here at Ferris State University. In both cases, however, the skills training workshops are attached to the content course, as a lab would be to a science course, and the workshop facilitator is someone who has taken, or is currently taking, the course. In addition, students are given instruction in how to apply the learning skills directly to the content of the course, resulting in a near transfer effect.

Not only does the content course provide an authentic environment for learning and applying learning skills and study strategies, but it also provides great incentive, since students need to learn these skills to be successful in the course. Teaching students to learn on their own is one of the most valuable gifts a teacher can give them, and the best place to do this is in our own classrooms.

Why Are Students Unprepared to Learn on Their Own?

Many faculty, when presented with the concept of teaching students to learn independently, affirm the importance and usefulness of this approach, but express doubt about its implementation since their students are often not even doing the reading, assignments, and homework they are currently given. These teachers rightfully wonder how they can possibly get their students to take on more responsibility for their own learning. The three examples that follow will shed some light on our students' current inability to learn on their own and provide guidelines for teachers about ways to cultivate and improve students' independent learning abilities.

1. Students don't do their reading and other assigned prep work because, based on their learning experience, they believe that teachers will discuss any important information included in the reading during class lectures. Students reason that there is no need to spend time doing the reading when the teacher is sure to fill them in on the important parts.

   When I facilitate faculty learning communities, I ask the faculty to identify one student from their subject area who can consult with them about the new teaching ideas they are considering for implementation. Our community then invites these students to spend one session with us, sharing their thoughts and ideas about teaching and learning. During this sharing session, faculty members always ask the students why they think their peers are not completing their reading assignments. The nearly unanimous answer, and this comes from some very bright and motivated learners, is that students don't read the material because they feel confident the teacher will always review the important points in the textbook during lecture. They often add a comment about teachers loving to talk. A simple fix to this problem would be to stop talking about the readings in a way that provides a review of their key ideas and concepts. However, this may not be practical, given the complexity and difficult of some of the readings. One possible solution is to place a higher value—remember, value equals grading—on completion of the readings by requiring written summaries, giving quizzes, or asking the students to lead classroom discussions of the readings. Another solution is to be sure we are assigning only readings that are really important for the students to read. This will make it clear that we are not assigning reading as busywork, and that the reading is essential to their learning.

2. Students don't do particularly well learning on their own because they have had little practice doing it in meaningful ways. Much of their independent work has been in the form of highly directed homework with a surface learning outcome attached to it. This kind of homework is what psychologist William Glasser (1990) calls "leaning on your shovel work." This kind of work does not challenge them, nor does it require them to develop effective independent learning skills, and students quickly realize its uselessness.

    If we are to help our students develop their independent learning skills, we must give them meaningful and challenging activities that require them to use the four areas of task management outlined earlier. When we do this, students can become active agents in the learning process and realize the importance and satisfaction associated with independent learning.

3. Students don't do well learning on their own because they have never had the opportunity to develop the skills needed to be effective independent learners. It is our job as teachers to direct and guide students in the development of independent learning skills. Through our learner-centered methods and our constant encouragement and explanation, students will understand the rationale behind our approach and will assume more responsibility for their own learning.

Helping Students Develop the Skills Needed to Learn on Their Own

I have identified eight skill areas that will allow students to become better at learning on their own. In every classroom we will find a few students who are fairly proficient in some of these areas; however, most students will need help to acquire and practice these important skills. The particular skills needed will vary from task to task, but the following list is a good representation of the most valuable general skills.

- Finding and evaluating quality sources of information
- Identifying important information in quality sources
- Organizing information in meaningful ways
- Writing reports and papers
- Managing time
- Remembering what has been learned
- Using problem-solving systems
- Monitoring one's own learning (metacognition)

You'll likely want to add other skills that are relevant to your particular course/subject. The skills listed above are core skills that apply to general course learning.

Skill One: Finding and Evaluating Quality Sources of Information

The five traditional criteria for evaluating print and media materials are:

- accuracy;
- authority;
- coverage;
- currency; and
- objectivity.

Finding and evaluating quality sources of information requires the ability to use these five criteria. Almost every college and university has guidelines to help students learn how to find and evaluate sources effectively. An extremely important part of this process is knowing the proper way to cite sources. Reviewing these five criteria with students before major independent learning activities, will, over time, greatly enhance their ability to become confident independent learners

Another way to assist students in developing these skills is to have them seek out a librarian and discuss how and where to find reliable sources of information. You might also invite a librarian into your class to give a workshop on using search engines, distinguishing between reputable and unsubstantiated information sources, and introducing students to the intricate world of specialized and subject area databases and search engines beyond such general ones as Google

You have probably already used most of the suggestions I offered here for teaching skill one. However, my purpose for starting with this skill area is to reinforce the fact that becoming proficient in finding and evaluating information is extremely important for successful independent learning. Students will only develop this crucial proficiency if this skill is taught, retaught, and reviewed continuously. Navigating the ever-expanding world of information is an activity in which our students will be engaged for the rest of their lives. Having the ability to do this capably and independently is one of the most valuable lifelong learning skills they will possess.

Skill Two: Identifying Important Information in Quality Sources

Many students have limited reading skills. A March 2006 study conducted by the American College Testing Program (ACT) reported that only 51% of college-bound students who took the ACT college entrance exam were prepared for college-level reading. Nationally, over 6 million American students in grades 6 through 12 are at risk of failure because they read and comprehend below—often considerably below—the basic levels needed for success in high school, postsecondary education, and the workforce. Only 30% of all secondary students read proficiently (Short & Fitzsimmons, 2007, p. 5).

The issue is not only that many college students are less-than-proficient readers, but, also, that those who read well have often learned to focus on surface issues rather than on the in-depth analysis required for independent learning. I often hear faculty complain about their students' reading abilities and vocabularies. They complain that the public schools don't require enough reading, that students do little pleasure reading on their own, and that students do not possess solid reading skills as a result. I certainly don't have a universal solution to the nation's reading problems; however, as a reading teacher, I can offer some helpful suggestions about how each of us, in our own classrooms, can help our students improve their reading skills, making them better able to learn on their own.

Setting a Purpose for the Reading

Anyone who is a skilled reader knows that to find what you are looking for in any piece of writing, but especially in a textbook, you must have a clear purpose in mind. The purpose is the guiding light that directs you as you determine what to pay attention to, and what to skip or skim. Many of our students have been taught that every word, sentence, and section requires equal attention. Teachers have reinforced this unhelpful idea by making such comments as, "everything in the chapter is important" or "the whole chapter is fair game for the test." These unfortunate statements cause students, even the most responsible ones, to become highly inefficient readers who feel they must read every single word to guard against being tested on some miniscule detail. (In my own high school history class, Sister Ann Francine used to ask test questions from the captions under the pictures in the textbook.) For those students who are already less inclined to complete their reading assignments, the idea of reading every single word overwhelms them and makes it even less likely that they will pick up their books. If our students could learn to read efficiently, and with a clear purpose in mind, they would be less inclined to skip the reading entirely, and more inclined to read it, skipping the material that is unimportant.

Initially, we should provide the purpose for our students' reading. Stating the purpose and modeling how a skilled reader uses a purpose to focus his or her reading is a great first step in improving their skills.

We must be sure, however, that the purpose will lead to more than a surface understanding of the material. For example, the following purposes, which are often assigned in teacher-centered classrooms, do not promote long-lasting learning and independent thinking:

- Read the chapter and answer the questions at the end.
- Read the chapter and outline each of the four units.
- Read the chapter and prepare 3 × 5 note cards on all technical vocabulary with definitions.

These examples of traditional purposes, which students are quite accustomed to receiving, direct students in very defined and narrow ways. Although they guide the reader and focus his or her attention, they do not help the reader develop a deep understanding of the topic. They completely ignore the most important skills a reader can possess, including identifying important concepts, facts, and details; figuring out why this information is important; and applying this information to the larger subject matter of the course to solve problems and/or make connections to a larger framework.

A purpose with the potential to lead to deeper learning might be: Read unit one of chapter 6 and be prepared to explain the concept of war as it was viewed by the American soldiers and how you think this concept might be viewed differently by Native American Indians.

If we are to optimize our students' opportunities to learn, we need to make it clear that reading every word is not the point. Skilled readers are able to use their purpose to decide what can be skipped or skimmed. In most college-level textbooks, 30–50% of the text consists of examples. Examples are important, since the author is not available to explain things to the students as they read. However, if a reader understands the main ideas and significant details, then the examples become less important. By learning to skip or skim the examples when the main point is already understood, a reading assignment that may have taken an hour will take only 40 minutes. Students who know how to do this become more efficient readers and trust that their teachers are more interested in their ability to grasp important points, than to be swallowed up in a flurry of details.

Helping Students Find the Main Ideas and Significant Details in Their Readings

For those students who need a little extra help to determine the important points in reading materials, here are some simple guidelines.

1. Turn headings and subheadings into questions and read the material to find the answers to these questions. The answer will almost always be the main idea.

   The following is a paragraph on the use of a Human Treasure Hunt as an icebreaker exercise. After reading it, look at the questions that follow as examples of the kinds of questions our students can use to guide their reading.

   > **Human Treasure Hunt**—this exercise not only requires the participants to get up on their feet and meet and greet each other, but it can also be written in a way so that it reveals any of a variety of information about the audience. The rules are simple. Each person

is handed a sheet of paper with 15 questions related to the hobbies and personal experiences of the group. Each person's job is to find at least two people who have these hobbies or have done the activities listed on the form by meeting each person in the group and asking him or her about the items listed. Examples would be, "Have you taught outside the United States?" or "Have you traveled to China?" or "Do you play golf?" The activity takes about 15 minutes to complete. When all the questions are answered, each item on the list is read aloud and all who have answered, "Yes," to the question are acknowledged. In this way, the new faculty discovers additional connections between themselves and others in the group. (Doyle & Marcinkiewicz, 2004)

The topic Human Treasure Hunt *can be turned into questions that can guide the reader. What is a Human Treasure Hunt? What is it used for? How does it work? Why would I use it? What might I learn from using it? Answering these questions provides the reader with a clear purpose for his or her reading, which is to locate the main ideas.*

2. There is great consistency in college textbook writing. As a result, as much as 90% of the time, the first sentence of a paragraph is the main idea. If the main idea is not found in the first sentence of a paragraph, the next likely spot is the last sentence. You should share this simple structural guide to finding main ideas with your students.

3. There are two simple guiding questions that can direct students to the main ideas when no headings are available:

   • Whom or what is the author writing about?
   • What is it that the author wants you to know about the who or the what?

This basic information will focus students on the important main ideas in their readings.

The definition of learner-centered practice—to optimize learning opportunities—allows us to view reading assignments in a different light. With this in mind, the goal of reading becomes to find and deeply understand the most important ideas and information in the most efficient way possible. This should be our students' purpose for reading. When we do our own research, because we are skilled readers, we automatically focus on just the information that meets our purpose. We do not waste our precious time reading material that does help us complete our task. We need to help our students develop the same reading skills. One final note to keep in mind about students' reading skills is that studies show that reading information from a computer screen can be as much as 30% slower than reading from a printed page (DeBra, 1996; Wright & Lickorish, 1983).

Skill Three: Organizing Information in Meaningful Ways

What we most often ask students to do when they work on their own is to organize their findings into well-written reports or papers. One of the best ways to help students organize information in meaningful ways is to show them organizational patterns that are commonly used to display information and let them practice fitting their information into these formats. For example, if we want students to address the similarities and differences between the Vietnam War and the war in Iraq, we might show them a chart illustrating the similarities and differences between the Revolutionary War and the Civil War. The categories in the chart, including causes, duration, causalities, weaponry, strategy, and cost, will show students the value of using meaningful categories to organize information and will give them ideas for their own organizational structure.

Organizational patterns, such as timelines and summaries, and hierarchal structures, such as personnel flow charts and outlines, are easy for students to use and easy for us to teach. Two important tools to master as students become proficient in organizing and reporting on their work are concept mapping and report and paper writing.

Concept Mapping

Concept mapping has been proven to help learners learn, help researchers create new knowledge, help administrators to better structure and manage organizations, and help writers to write and evaluators to assess learning (Novak & Cañas, 2006). Mapping is perhaps the most powerful of all organizational structures for ease of learning. It not only identifies the relationships between ideas, it organizes them from biggest to smallest or most important to least important, and it displays this information in a visual format. When students can see the relationships and connections between different pieces of information, the ideas and facts become much easier to remember (Zull, 2002, p. 145).

Concept mapping is the process of identifying important concepts, arranging the concepts spatially, identifying relationships among the concepts, and labeling the nature of the semantic relationships among the concepts. Mapping is a way of organizing information that enhances students' thinking and retention (Novack & Cañas, 2006). Studies have shown that students engage in some of their best thinking when they try to represent something graphically, and thinking is a necessary condition for learning (Jonassen, 1996). Experiments have shown that students using concept mapping outperform those who do not use it in longer-term retention tests (Novak, Gowin, & Johansen, 1983).

Constructivist learning theory states that new knowledge needs be integrated into existing structures to be remembered and receive meaning. Concept mapping stimulates this process by making the new knowledge, and its connections to background knowledge, explicit by requiring the learner to notice the relationship between concepts (Plotnick, 1996). Teaching students mapping skills will provide them with an organizational structure they can use in almost any learning situation.

Uses of Concept Mapping

Representing knowledge in the visual format of a concept map allows one to gain an overview of a domain of knowledge (Plotnick, 1996). This can be used to generate ideas (brainstorming), design complex structures (long texts, hypermedia, large websites), communicate complex ideas, aid learning by explicitly integrating new and old knowledge, and assess understanding or diagnose misunderstanding (Lanzing, 1997). As a way of organizing information mapping has several advantages:

- Visual symbols are quickly and easily recognized.
- Minimum use of text makes it easy to scan for a word, phrase, or the general idea.
- Visual representation allows for development of a holistic understanding that words alone cannot convey (Plotnick, 1996).

Making a Concept Map

The first characteristic of a concept map is that the concepts are represented in a hierarchical fashion, with the most inclusive, most general concepts at the top of the map and the more specific, less general concepts arranged hierarchically below. The second characteristic is the inclusion of cross-links.

These are relationships or links between concepts in different segments or domains of the concept map. Cross-links help students see how a concept in one domain of knowledge represented on the map is related to a concept in another. Figure 5.1 is a concept map of learner-centered teaching. Notice how the map is ordered from biggest to smallest and how it clearly displays the divisions within the information.

Additional benefits of concept mapping include:

- Concept maps organize, enhance, and encourage understanding.
- They help students learn new information by having them integrate each new idea into their existing body of knowledge.
- As students create concept maps, they reiterate ideas using their own words, causing them to relearn the material in a more familiar way.
- Misdirected links or wrong connections alert educators to what students do not understand. (Novak & Cañas, 2006)

FIGURE 5.1
Map of roles.

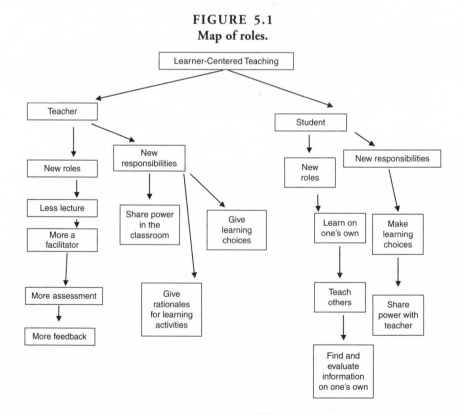

By teaching our students mapping, we give them a powerful tool for organizing and communicating the information they learn from their firsthand activities.

Skill Four: Writing Reports and Papers

If I had to decide whether faculty complain more about their students' poor reading or poor writing skills, I would have to pick writing. Even my daughter, a teaching assistant in her MFA program, called to tell me that her first-year students can't write. She asked, "How can these kids be in college with these poor writing skills?"

I am not suggesting that we all become writing teachers, but we can teach and model some basic organizational skills for our students that will help them prepare the written reports and papers we assign. These organizational models will not cure their grammar errors or syntax problems, but they will provide an effective structure to enable students to produce well-organized reports and papers.

Most colleges and universities have writing centers or professional development websites that include guidelines for writing different types of reports. These sites are excellent sources for students who need help with their writing assignments. I have included two examples of effective writing structures in appendix A. The first is a structure for a research report, the second is for writing a paper from information found in reading assignments. Directing students to these kinds of structural guidelines, combined with some instruction on conducting research projects, will go a long way toward improving students' performance and skills.

Skill Five: Managing Time

I have been teaching time management skills to college students for the past 30 years. I've discovered that students need a three-pronged approach to develop an effective system of managing their time. The first approach is a philosophical one. Students must develop a philosophy about using their time. To help them with this, I have relied on Alan Lakein's simple definition of time: "Time is Life. To waste your time is to waste your life but to value your time is to value your life" (1974). When students take an abstract idea like time and make it concrete and personal, they begin to view time management in a new way. They start to understand that life is not a dress rehearsal.

In the second part of the approach, I teach students how to determine which, of all possible uses of time, are the most important and should be given priority. This process includes a discussion of setting goals, identifying personal values, and determining high priorities. Establishing these three determiners of time use gives students a way of looking at their current life situation and assessing the importance of various activities. I make it quite clear that decisions about how we use our time can, and do, change as life situations change.

To illustrate how to make effective use of time, I use the example of running out of clean clothes. I point out that doing laundry becomes a high priority when you run out of clean clothes, but being out of clean clothes should not let laundry take priority over studying for tomorrow's math test. The decision to study and wear dirty clothes would be logical and appropriate based on the values and priorities the students set for college success. By maintaining college as a high priority at all times, students have a firm basis for making time management decisions when issues, needs, and options other than school intervene.

The third approach involves teaching students to use the tools of time management. We discuss the use of planners, calendars, alarm clocks, Post-it notes, to-do lists, Palm Pilots, and friends and family to manage time. We are all busy people, and it's common to have as many as 10 different things to accomplish in any one day. The particular tools a person chooses to manage his or her daily tasks is a personal decision. However, thinking you can remember all of your assignments, test dates, due dates, social dates, and personal commitments without recording them is bound to result in missed dates and deadlines and the resulting consequences.

This three-part approach provides students with

- a clear rationale for improving their time management, (if you waste your time, you waste your life);
- a system to make time management decisions; and
- suggestions for tools to assist with managing time and keeping track of dates and deadlines.

Sharing this process with your students will sharpen their time management skills, which becomes increasingly important as we ask them to do more learning on their own. To access a downloadable PowerPoint presentation that details these three areas see: http://www.ferris.edu/htmls/aca

demics/center/Teaching_and_Learning_Tips/T_LHome.htm and click on "Time Management (powerpoint)."

Skill Six: Remembering What Has Been Learned

> The fact is that you cannot forget something that you never truly learned.
>
> —Sprenger, 2005

> Cramming seeks to stamp things in by intense application immediately before the ordeal. But a thing thus learned can form but few associations.
>
> —James, 2000

It is not a pleasant feeling to put a great deal of effort into a task and have nothing to show for it. The same is true for putting effort into learning something new and then not being able to recall it. Although psychologists and neuroscientists are far from completely understanding how human memory operates, there is some very important research about memory that can help students reap long-term dividends from their learning efforts.

Researchers and cognitive neuroscientists have identified a blend of factors (Arendal & Mann, 2000) that can lead to learning new tasks and concepts successfully. Sprenger (2005) outlined these:

- Frequency: Neural pathways grow strong by repeated exposure to learning. The more our students practice, review, discuss, write, and reflect on what they are learning, the stronger the neural pathways for recall become.
- Intensity: Learning requires rigorous practice. A student will build neural support for a skill in less time if the practice is intense.
- Cross-training: Teaching for memory means building strong networks that can connect to other networks. Different kinds of skills and different forms of memory will trigger these connections. For example, having students read, write, and discuss a topic builds stronger networks than using any only of these modes.
- Adaptivity: The ability to recognize whether the memory system being used is working effectively and, if not, changing to another form of memory formation, is key to successful recall. Students need to learn how to monitor their own memory systems by paying attention

to how hard or easy it is for them to recall information when using a particular mode of learning.

- Motivation and attention: Frequency and intensity depend on the students being attentive and motivated to do the learning (Sprenger, 1995, p. 7). Explaining to students repeatedly why assignments and class activities are crucial to their current and future learning and career goals is a key to keeping students engaged and motivated to learn.

Collectively, these five factors can lead to improved memory formation and recall. Students can also work toward improving their ability to recall information. Several strategies for helping students achieve as much recall as possible are outlined below.

Seeing the Connections Between Comprehension and Recall

Unclear information has little chance of making its way into long-term memory. It is true that a person who does not read Greek can memorize a poem written in Greek and recall the whole poem when asked to do so. However, the recall is limited exclusively to the Greek words themselves, in the exact order in which they were learned. Because the person does not comprehend the poem's meaning, all the other possible cues that could help to recall the poem, such as thinking about other poems with similar meanings or themes, are unavailable to them. The person cannot connect the poem to his or her background knowledge because the person does not understand Greek.

Recalling information is deeply tied to our ability to attach that information to our experiences and existing knowledge. For students to make those attachments, they must understand the skills and knowledge they are being asked to learn. If our students nod their heads like bobble-head dolls when we ask if they understand the material, but they really don't understand it, they are greatly limiting their chances for recall. The brain learns by looking for patterns of similarity between the sensory data it receives and the data already stored within it (Ratey, 2002, p. 55). The brain cannot make connections to already-held patterns if it cannot recognize the sensory data. The data simply have no place to go. When students don't understand and don't ask for help, their efforts at memory formation are sure to be unsuccessful.

Using Emotions to Aid Memory Formation

Everyday experiences and laboratory studies reveal that emotionally charged incidents are better remembered than nonemotional events. Emotions boost attention and elaboration, which strongly influence whether an experience will be remembered (Schacter, 2001, p. 163). When the amygdala detects emotion, the areas of the brain that form memories are stimulated (Hamann, Ely, Grafton, & Kilts, 1999). Learning is a social and emotional process as well as a cognitive one. When students can use their emotions to build memories, they possess a tool that will greatly aid their independent learning.

In most cases, finding personal emotional connections to the information will aid memory formations; try these helpful hints:

- When possible, pick a topic of great interest to research or learn about.
- Connect the information with a story—the brain loves stories (Caine & Caine 1994).
- Connect the learning to visual images that have emotional content.

Reflecting on What Has Been Learned

Reflection is a combination of intellectual and affective activities in which we engage to explore our experiences, leading to a new understanding (Boud, Keogh, & Walker, 1985). Reflection is about examining learning from various angles and in various lights to make certain nothing has been missed or overlooked (Dewey, 1997). Reflection is a powerful instrument for students in that it triggers background connections for new information being learned. Reflecting on how the information can be applied, or how it affirms or conflicts with previously held information, promotes deeper understanding and strengthens the connections to knowledge and information already stored in the brain. The reflection process also increases the number of cues students can call on, making it much more likely that they will be successful in making relevant connections and retrieving the desired information. When a student fails to answer our questions, it might be due to our questions and cues, not to a lack of knowledge on the student's part. As teachers, we must think carefully about our role in asking questions and providing cues that optimize our students' learning. The more connections students can make, the more likely they will be able to respond to our cues successfully.

Reflection activities can be general, for example, asking students to think about how the new information they learned might help them solve a problem in their own lives. They can also be very specific, like asking students to think about how today's new information might change the answer they gave for yesterday's case study. Reflection can also be a shared activity. When students share their reflections with one another, everyone involved examines his or her own thoughts and ideas more carefully, leading to affirmation for some and adjustment for others.

Recoding What Has Been Learned

A great way to see if students have understood new information is to ask them to explain it in their own words. This is called recoding. The recoding process reveals whether students completely understood the information. If the students cannot explain the material in their own words, or if they can't think of useful examples or analogies, they probably do not have a clear understanding of it. This means that creating memories for it will be difficult. When students are able to explain, in their own words, what they have learned, they are expanding the connections for that information by linking it to the most familiar and easiest language to recall, their own.

One effective tool to help students put information into their own words is summary writing. It is also beneficial to provide students with a model summary that clearly illustrates what we expect in their finished product.

The Power of Reviewing

Information needs to be used regularly, over an extended period, to become a part of long-term memory (Sprenger, 2005). Students need to understand that there is almost no long-term retention without review and rehearsal (Sousa, 2001, p. 86). Reviews do not require long periods, but they are essential for retention. As time passes, daily reviews of well-practiced material can be decreased to once every few days and still be effective (Schenck, 2001). Consistent review also prevents blocking, which is when information is stored but cannot be accessed, and guards against misattribution, attributing a memory to the wrong source, and transience, the fading of memories over time. In *Seven Sins of Memory*, Daniel Schacter (2001) describes these three "sins" as the most common pitfalls for students.

Sleep and Memory

We must make our students aware of the importance of sleep. Many top researchers in the memory field agree that memories are encoded during sleep (Schacter, 1996; Stickgold, 2000; Mitru, Millrood, & Mateika, 2002). Students who sleep only six hours remember far less than those who sleep eight (Stickgold, 2000).

Skill Seven: Using Problem-Solving Systems

Ask any employer, recruiter, or program advisory board member which skills he or she expects college graduates to have, and problem-solving skills will be high on the list. Ask teachers and cognitive psychologists what types of learning activities will help develop the thinking skills of students, and solving problems will be high on the list of answers as well. Ask college faculty where in the curriculum problem-solving skills are taught, and the answer should be in every course. However, the truth is that most faculty are not certain where students learn these important skills (other than in their own courses). If students are to be effective independent learners, we must teach them how to solve problems on their own. I have already addressed some of the skills they need earlier in this chapter. Finding important information, evaluating sources, and organizing information are all important components of solving problems.

Our job is to design authentic problems and help our students learn how to examine and solve them on their own. I have included a list of excellent websites in appendix B for teaching problem solving and for developing cases and problems for students to solve. Also included in appendix B is a generic example of a process that is commonly used to guide learners through a problem-solving activity.

Educators have spent a great deal of time creating problems to bolster problem-solving skills. Resources, which abound in every subject area, can be called on to provide your students with authentic problem-solving activities.

Skill Eight: Monitoring One's Own Learning (Metacognition)

It is important not to do too much thinking for your students. When you think for them, your students will become experts at seeking help, rather than expert thinkers (Biemiller & Meichenbaum, 1992).

Metacognition refers to learners' automatic awareness of their own knowledge and their ability to understand, control, and manipulate their own cognitive processes. Metacognitive skills are important not only in school, but throughout life (Vockell, 2006); they are a key component in independent learning. Chapter 10 provides a complete discussion of metacognition.

We Need to Help Make Our Students More Independent Learners

When I work with faculty who are frustrated by the lack of skills their students possess, I tell them they can complain about it or they can fix the problem. My own frustrations as a teacher were greatly reduced years ago, when I accepted that my job was to teach the students who were sitting in my class, not those I wished were sitting there. If we want our students to take on new roles and responsibilities, we have to help them build the skill sets to make this possible. Getting our students to work on their own is a crucial part of this process. Teaching them how to work effectively with others is also important and is detailed in the next chapter.

6

COMMUNICATION SKILLS FOR WORKING WITH PEERS

Knowing and learning are communal acts. They require many eyes and ears, many observations and experiences. They require a continual cycle of discussion, disagreement, and consensus over what has been seen and what it all means.

—Palmer, 1990

Learning is enhanced when teachers pay attention to the knowledge and beliefs that learners bring to the learning task; use this knowledge as a starting point for new instruction.

—Bransford et al., 2000, p. 11

W hat do our students know about working effectively with other students? What have their previous experiences taught them about how groups and teams work? What concerns do they have about working with others? Finding the answers to these questions is the best place to start building a successful model of students' cooperation, collaboration, and teamwork.

I first became familiar with an excellent activity that can provide the insights we need into our students' attitudes about working with others, as well as their abilities to do so, when Maryellen Weimer, author of *Learner-Centered Teaching* (2002), visited our campus in 2003. I have continued to refine this activity and find it is a great place to begin our discussion about getting students to work with one another more effectively. The activity has seven steps:

1. Have students meet in groups of three to discuss their responses to the following questions:

    - In your experience as a learner, what are the characteristics, behaviors, or attitudes that made the times you were asked to work with others one-on-one or in specific groups or teams effective and valuable learning experiences?
    - In your experience as a learner, what are the characteristics, behaviors, or attitudes that made the times you were asked to work with others one-on-one or in specific groups or teams unsuccessful, unproductive, or difficult learning experiences?

2. Designate one student to record all the characteristics, behaviors, and attitudes the group members identify.

3. Have each group share its findings with the whole class, one finding per group at a time until all findings have been identified. Record the findings on the whiteboard (a smart board would be great for this activity).

4. Have the students return to their groups and ask them to develop an effective set of ground rules for working with others on assignments and projects using the answers from the two questions as a guide. The ground rules or guidelines should be statements that will help ensure that effective and valuable learning experiences occur and prevent unsuccessful, unproductive, or difficult ones. An example of a guideline is that each member of the group or class must contribute to the discussion.

5. Make a master list of the ground rules, refining and combining similar ground rules as necessary.

6. Take the list home, edit it for clarity, and add any important ideas the students have left out. Bring the list back to class the next day.

7. Tell the students that each of the ideas represents a "plank" of the ground rules for working with others in the class, and have the students vote on each "plank." Unless the planks are counterproductive to classroom learning, the teacher should not veto any of them.

This exercise allows students to make choices collectively and give input about an area of learning that can be emotionally charged for many. Working with others requires students to reveal parts of themselves that they could otherwise keep hidden from their peers. This is no small issue for students.

This exercise also reveals what our students think works and does not work when they are asked to work in groups. Finally, this exercise allows our students to be the main architects of the guidelines for working with others, which means they will have to take responsibility for using them. Getting students to take on this kind of responsibility is an important outcome of a learner-centered process.

Research on Working With Others

The often-used cliché, "Two heads are better than one," has some very good research behind it. Certainly, working with others is not always productive, but dozens of research studies point to numerous benefits to learners who engage with others in discussion, problem-solving activities, and course projects. For example, Springer, Stanne, and Donovan (1997) conducted a meta-analysis of 39 studies of small-group learning in science, math, engineering, and technology courses. They found that small-group learning is effective in promoting greater academic achievement, more favorable attitudes toward learning, and increased persistence in courses and programs. Figure 6.1 lists some of the benefits students gain from working and discussing ideas with others.

Working With Others Is Often Not a Learning Priority

Effective collaboration requires a skill that most students have not mastered—speaking. One reason why students lack this skill is that, of the three main modes our students use to learn—writing, reading, and speaking—the

FIGURE 6.1
Benefits of working with others.

- Improves students intellectually
- Stimulates interest in learning
- Increases confidence in intellectual and social abilities
- Improves understanding of group dynamics
- Helps students learn to express feelings
- Can help build assertiveness skills
- Enhances awareness of diverse views and ideas
- Exposes students to different ways of thinking
- Validation of already held ideas and beliefs

one least used is speaking (Nystrand & Gamoran, 1991b). In addition, many teachers do not require students who are shy about or uncomfortable with speaking to do it. The irony is that speaking to others is one of the most important, if not *the* most important, professional and personal skill students must have to be successful in their lives and careers. I find it contradictory that institutions of higher education would never dream of allowing students who cannot read and write effectively to graduate, but they do allow students who have done little or no speaking in their classes to graduate.

I am not trying to be insensitive to students who are challenged by talking openly in classroom discussions or prefer to work alone. However, I do want to emphasize the need for them to understand that learning the skills required to work with others is crucial to being well educated, even when these skills make them uncomfortable and are not a preferred learning style. Many who teach in higher education view the skills needed to interact effectively with others as less important than other skills students need. The fact is that most professionals spend a significant amount of time on a day-to-day basis communicating and working with others, often much more time than they spend reading or writing. Therefore, we must enhance the use of learning activities that require our students to communicate and work effectively with others. Studies by Nystrand and Gamoran (1991a) clearly demonstrate that "discussions among students of subject matter are highly correlated with student achievement, even though they don't happen very often in a college classroom. We need to ensure that these interactions happen on a more regular basis in our classrooms.

The Rationale for Students Working With Others

The rationale for students working effectively with others is a simple one: if they cannot learn to work well with others, their professional success will be in jeopardy. The following four reality checks should help students see the need to embrace communication skills:

1. In the workplace, not knowing how to express your ideas clearly and accurately to others, or how to listen carefully to their needs, can be career threatening.
2. Ideas, suggestions, questions, or concerns will not be heard in the world of work if you wait to be called on. You must learn how to

speak up and assert your views and ideas; the real world is not a passive learning environment.

3. Getting the attention of the leadership or those whom you work with at any level of your organization will depend on your ability to present ideas quickly, clearly, and effectively. Time is a commodity that is not doled out in large chunks by busy people.

4. If you do not learn to listen carefully to what the customer, client, patient, coworker, or boss has to say, you will be jeopardizing your professional credibility.

Being able to offer one's views in clear and concise ways and listen carefully and attentively when working with others are among the most important and valued skills of any professional. If we could follow our graduates around as they begin their professional careers, we would find, almost regardless of career, that they spend a great deal of their time talking and listening to their customers, clients, patients, peers, employees, and bosses. Engaging in these interactions effectively is crucial to their success.

Helping Students See Past the Problems of Working With Others

Despite research supporting the numerous benefits of working with others, many students still do not look forward to group work. The reasons behind their concerns, beyond their personal experiences, are spelled out in a comprehensive review, titled "Surviving the Group Project: A Note on Working in Teams," developed at Northeastern University (2006). The findings of this review indicate that groups struggle for the following reasons:

- *A weak sense of direction.* Students need to understand that working in groups or teams means they have to learn how to set reasonable goals, define a purpose for their work, and share leadership roles. A lack of focus, purpose, goals, approach, and leadership will lead to failure.
- *Infighting.* It is not essential that members like each other, but they do need to respect one another. Group members need to learn how to manage their disagreements and conflicts, set aside petty differences, and compromise for the betterment of the group.

- *Shirking of responsibilities.* Students need to learn how to assign tasks and responsibilities fairly and in a way that reflects the strengths of group members. Failure of members to take on their fair share of responsibilities creates a pseudo team that is likely to underperform.
- *Lack of trust.* Students need to learn to trust one another. This can be achieved by spending time getting to know one another before embarking on a graded task together.
- *Critical skills gaps.* Students need to learn how to deal with conflicts, manage tasks, communicate with each other, make group decisions, and organize task duties, and we must help them to develop these skills. Even the most cooperative teams will still have difficulties if they lack these skills.
- *Lack of external support.* Students depend on us to provide the directions, resources, framework, and methods of accountability; timelines; rubric/grading system; and a meaningful and authentic task for the members to work on. Students also need to be assured that we will do our part.

By explaining the problems of group work, and how they can be resolved, we can alleviate our students' concerns, making them more likely to accept such work.

Helping Students Learn the Elements of Effective Group Work

Katzenbach and Smith (1993) characterize effective groups as groups where individual and mutual accountability and a sense of common commitment exist among all members. Whether they are "leaders" or not, the members take responsibility for the group's effectiveness and for dealing with the inevitable problems that arise. The best teams invest a tremendous amount of time and effort exploring, shaping, and agreeing on a purpose that belongs to all of the members, collectively and individually, and then translate this purpose into specific performance goals. The key elements that can help our students to work effectively in groups include:

- Students must have enough background knowledge and learning skills to handle the assigned tasks. We must be sure the tasks assigned are developmentally appropriate.

- Students need to set a norm for their group. Norms play a significant role in the success of student groups, so we need to help students see the value of norms and encourage them to agree on a stated, positive norm for their group, such as "Everyone does his or her own share," and not on a norm that will undermine the success of the group, such as "Let's get this completed as quickly as possible."

- Students need to facilitate group cohesiveness. Group members should be given the time and activities to build connections among themselves. Making personal choices to accept and get along with other members leads to greater cooperation and productivity.

- Students need to understand that their own personal success can come about only through the group's success. Knowing that your peers are relying on you is a powerful motivator for group work (Kohn, 1986). Students need to see that what will be evaluated is not only completing the task, but the effectiveness of the group members in working together to reach that goal.

- Students need to learn that facts and hard evidence, not opinion and wishful thinking, are crucial to getting group members to agree on a particular solution or point of view. Forming subgroups is less likely to occur in groups that learn how to gather data and research findings effectively to solve the assigned problem or task.

- Students need to learn how to give constructive criticism and meaningful feedback to one another. This is one of the most important aspects of working with others and a lifelong learning skill they will need to be successful in their professions. However, many students lack this skill. Many websites offer excellent guidelines for teaching students how to give feedback to their peers. Asking our students to visit these websites and then having them practice giving feedback in their groups would be a great learner-centered assignment.

Helping Students Learn How to Talk to Each Other

One of the most common forms of working with others is class discussions. These can be formal or informal, small- or large-group interactions designed to increase students' awareness and understanding of the issues of the course. Unfortunately, many students are reluctant to participate in class discussions. Here are some suggestions for getting our students more involved in talking with each other:

- We need to offer our students the opportunity to talk. We spend so much time talking that we often don't allow our students ample time to respond to our questions, instead providing the answers for them. We are too interested in keeping a certain pace for our class. It is time for us to start listening and stop talking so much.

- We need to get students to see the value of discussions. Students have learned that what is important to the teacher is graded. Because discussions usually are not graded, students believe they are not important to the teacher, which gives them little reason to participate. If we grade discussions, students are more likely to take them seriously. A method for grading discussions is outlined later in this chapter.

- We need to get students to see the connection between discussion and learning. To do so, we must explain to them how discussion leads to a deeper understanding of issues and concepts, and how it can help confirm ideas or beliefs or correct wrongly held beliefs or misunderstandings We must also explain that discussion teaches them to articulate their ideas clearly, organize and support their ideas and views, listen carefully, and give critical feedback in appropriate ways. Finally, we must explain that discussions help them see points of view they may not have considered, to be respectful of views they do not share, and to consider changing their views based on solid data and research presented by others.

- We need to allow our students a say in developing a set of guidelines for how discussions will be conducted. This can be done using the 7-step process outlined at the beginning of this chapter. Simply change the two questions. The first question would become, "What are the characteristics of the classroom discussions that were productive, interesting, and exciting? and the second question would become, "What are the characteristics of the classroom discussions that made them unproductive, uninteresting, or boring?" Using the information the students provide from this activity to develop guidelines for discussions will give them ownership of making class discussions more productive. Figure 6.2 provides a list of questions to help students develop guidelines for discussions.

- We need to make our students feel comfortable about speaking in class. Students may be shy, English may be their second language, or they may simply be better at writing their ideas than at saying them. Allowing students time to prepare for discussions and giving them the

FIGURE 6.2
Questions to help students formulate guidelines for discussions.

- Who gets to participate in the discussion? Do students have to have read the assignment or completed the homework to participate? If so, how will it be verified?
- How do students participate in the discussion? Must they raise their hands and be acknowledged by the professor, or can they just speak out when they have something to ask or add?
- What behaviors are acceptable when students challenge or disagree with one another?
- What language will be deemed inappropriate for classroom use based on current cultural norms?
- How should students be graded on their participation in the discussion?
- Are all forms of participating of equal value—that is, asking a question, responding to a question, giving a view, challenging an answer, expanding on an answer?
- What are the consequences for those who do not participate?
- Should there be a privacy rule, for example, "Anything discussed in the classroom stays in the classroom"?
- Should there be a time limit for speaking?
- Who should be responsible for keeping the discussion on track?

questions to be discussed in advance can boost their confidence and help them to become better contributors. It may also be helpful to allow students to write out their ideas and views and bring them to class so they can read from their notes if necessary.

- We need to ensure that students are prepared. This can be achieved by having them help set the guidelines for discussion. Giving students some say in the consequences of not being prepared gives them greater responsibility for being prepared.
- We need to give students time to think about what they are going to say so they can make intelligent and thoughtful contributions. This can be achieved by giving students the topics to be discussed beforehand and allowing them ample time to formulate a response in class before moving on to someone else. Typically, instructors wait in silence only about a half-second for a student to respond (Stahl, 1994). By increasing this wait time to 3 seconds, the number of student responses often increases dramatically (Rowe, 1974).
- We need to make our students feel that the classroom environment is safe and receptive to sharing views and ideas. Guidelines for discussion can address these concerns.

Research suggests that many more students want to talk in class than usually do. A study from the University of North Carolina Center for Teaching and Learning (1991) found that almost 30% of students responding to the study questionnaire reported they had wanted to speak in class but had not done so because they felt uncertain of their abilities. It is up to us to provide the encouragement they need to engage in our classroom discussions.

Grading Discussions

As I mentioned earlier, students often tie the value of what they are doing in the classroom to whether it is being graded. By providing our students with a fair and meaningful grading system for what they learn through discussion, we can help them understand just how important this aspect of learning is. Middendorf and Kalish (1996) offer these suggestions for grading discussions:

- Write a note to each student twice a semester telling the student his or her grade for participation and the basis for the grade. A rubric describing the value of various aspects of the discussion, such as preparedness, number of contributions, new information provided beyond that of the assigned readings, and new insights contributed, could be used to guide the grading process.
- Require a written product from students for their group activities and classroom discussions and grade it.
- Ask a significant number of questions on exams that are directly related to the classroom discussions.

We Make the Difference

To get our students to work together, we must provide a clear rationale for doing so. They need to see that working with others creates opportunities for enhanced learning, that the world in which they live is a world of collaboration, and that the ideas and solutions that may make or break their careers are likely to come from working with others. Finally, students need to know that we value working with others as a meaningful part of our courses.

7

HELPING STUDENTS TAKE
CHARGE OF THEIR LEARNING

An important facet of learning is "developing in learners the capacity to accept increasingly more responsibility for their learning" (Bickmore-Brand, 1996) As teachers, we need to support learners in this process, enabling them to take risks and learn from their mistakes.

Of the many teaching changes we must make when moving to a learner-centered approach, the most difficult may be to share power with our students over their learning. Ironically, this is also the best way to help them take charge of their own learning. We have been so conditioned by traditional teacher-centered approaches that invest teachers with all of the authority and control over the learning process, that giving away some of that power makes many of us uncomfortable. Our students also feel this discomfort when we ask them to take more control over their learning and assume responsibility for what and how they learn. For us to help our students feel comfortable in their new, more proactive role, we must first feel comfortable with the idea of sharing power and how to do so. The first half of this chapter focuses on the reasons for sharing power with our students; the second half identifies areas where student choice and control can be increased and provides suggestions for helping students make good choices and handle their increased responsibilities.

Teachers' Concerns About Sharing Power

Although we are committed to a learner-centered approach that includes sharing power with our students, we often still have concerns about what will happen if students have too much control, or if they make poor choices about their learning. After all, we all know that the accountability buck for what happens in our courses still stops with us.

The most common concerns faculty identify regarding sharing power include fear of losing control of the class, having to pick up the pieces when students make poor decisions or fail to take charge of their learning, and the added time it takes to develop and assess assignments and activities that allow for student choice. These are all reasonable concerns, born out of the teacher-centered environments in which we have spent most of our careers. I have developed four basic ideas that I believe will prove useful in alleviating our concerns over power sharing.

1. Our students cannot become more responsible learners unless we give them more responsibility. This is analogous to our children learning to drive. We can't help them become skilled and safe drivers if we never let them behind the wheel. It's scary, but it's the only way they will learn this new skill.

2. The more control our students take, and the more choices we offer them, the greater will be their desire and willingness to engage in the learning process (Zull, 2002, p. 52). It is human nature for people to want some control over what happens to them. Choices give our students some say in their learning process. When this occurs, students take more ownership of what they are learning (p. 52).

3. When students make a choice, they must learn to live with that choice; this is a very powerful life lesson. Choices obviate students' excuses.

4. When students have some control over how they learn, they will discover their strengths and weakness as learners, a vital metacognitive skill that will serve them throughout their lives. Faculty have also told me that students learn to exercise more thoughtful decision making when the decision affects their grade.

Students can learn many things from having choices. One of my colleagues decided she would give each of her students the choice between an in-class or a take-home exam. She thought that, for some of her students, a take-home exam might provide a better opportunity to explain what they had learned. Some of the students who chose the take-home exam discovered that it required more work than they'd expected, and they opted for an in-class exam for the next test. For others, however, even though the take-home exam was a lot of work, it really helped them to learn and understand the material. They also felt more confident in their ability as learners than they had in the past while studying for in-class exams. Whatever the outcome, the students learned something new about themselves as learners that they wouldn't have known had they not been given this simple choice.

Are Students Skilled Enough to Take Control?

On a national radio program, I heard Stephen Covey, author of *Seven Habits of Highly Effective People*, relate a conversation he had with his then-young son about keeping the clothes in his closet hung up on hangers. After a father-and-son heart-to-heart that concluded with the son's promise to take on this responsibility, Covey was dismayed when he once again found his son's clothes on the floor. When he confronted his son, he discovered that the boy did not know how to put clothes on hangers, something Covey assumed he knew how to do. This skill deficiency, not a lack of willingness to be responsible, was the cause of the messy closet. The message is a simple one: if we ask our students to take more control over their learning, we must be certain they have the skills to do so.

An important way to begin checking our students' skills is to ask them to identify their strengths and weaknesses as learners. Asking students to write about their strengths and weaknesses is a simple but highly effective way to assess their perceptions of themselves as learners.

We should also always ask about students' skill levels and familiarity when we are assigning learning tasks. When asking students to write a summary, it is important to confirm that they know what a summary contains. In my senior-level education course, I discovered that many of my students did not know (or did not remember) how to write a summary. Rather than being shocked, I reviewed the steps for doing so. The result was a pile of well-written assignments. Other important questions we must keep in mind include: What kind of teaching style do students like? Do they like to learn alone or with others or both ways? Are they already familiar with the course material, or do they have any personal life experience related to the course? Gathering as much information about our students as possible, including their background knowledge and their repertoire of learning skills, is the first step in giving them more control over their learning. We can only make them successful independent learners if we know what they are capable of doing for themselves. Gathering information from students is discussed more thoroughly in chapter 11.

Perhaps of equal importance to gathering this information is the positive message we send to our students just by taking the time to get it. By asking them to tell us what kinds of learners they are, we are illustrating our desire to ensure they have the skills and strategies they will need to be successful.

The Power of Choice in Learning

At a teaching conference in 2002, I heard an amazing story about the power of offering learning choices to students. The storyteller was Dr. Roger Taylor, a classroom teacher, administrator, professor, and internationally known educational consultant. The story had to do with an experience Dr. Taylor (2002) had while teaching an AP history class for the Chicago Public Schools in which he offers his students 100 different ways to show their understanding of the content being taught. One very shy young man in the class said nothing for the first three weeks. One day the young man approached Dr. Taylor and asked in a quiet, almost whispering way, "Can we really do a puppet show in this class?"

Dr. Taylor responded enthusiastically, "Yes, of course, it's one of the options on the syllabus." That was the entire conversation. Three weeks later, when Dr. Taylor arrived early for the 8 a.m. class, he found the shy young man in the classroom working, and learned that he had been there since 4 a.m. What Dr. Taylor saw was beyond his imagination—a wall full of computer recording equipment, speakers set out around the room, three tables covered in American flags, and carved wooden puppets of Abraham Lincoln and Frederick Douglass. When his classmates arrived, the young man proceeded to perform a puppet show of the first Lincoln-Douglass debate, complete with recordings he had made of all of the background noises that would have been present.

The performance was so impressive that Dr. Taylor, who videotapes all of his students' presentations, sent the tape to Steven Spielberg, who sent it on to George Lucas. As the story goes, Lucas was so impressed that he gave the student a college scholarship and wants the young man to work for him when he graduates. As educators, the message we must take from this story is that Dr. Taylor would have known nothing about the immense talents of this young man were it not for designing a syllabus that offered students such a wide range of creative choices to illustrate their grasp of the course material. Am I suggesting that we all include puppet shows on our syllabi? No . . . well, maybe. What I am suggesting is that giving our students more options to demonstrate what they have learned will lead to discoveries that just might blow us away. More important, in the process, our students will have taken an incredibly important step on their way to becoming successful, confident, independent learners.

What Message Are We Sending to Students When We Share Power?

At Ferris State, I have the great pleasure of working with our new faculty in a yearlong new faculty transition program. The first piece of advice about teaching that I give my new colleagues is to learn the names of their students as quickly as possible. Most realize the importance of doing this, but they also wonder why, of all the advice I could give them, I have chosen to deliver this piece first. My answer is simple. At its core, teaching is a human-to-human interaction. It is about forming positive working relationships with our students. Knowing a person's name is key to beginning that relationship. When we learn our students' names quickly, we are expressing our desire to get to know them. We are also sending a message of respect. Every decision we make about teaching sends a message to our students. When we fail to maintain order in the classroom, the message is that we don't really care about their learning. When we share power with our students by offering learning choices, the message is that we trust their judgment, and we are confident they will make decisions that are in their best interest, and in the best interest of the community of learners of which they are a part.

What Power Should Be Shared?

There are three major areas in which we can share power and offer students choices, without concern that we will lose control of the class or be seen as abdicating our responsibilities. They are the learning environment, learning tasks and assignments, and assessments of learning.

The Learning Environment

Our classrooms should be shared-learning environments in which the needs of both teacher and students are met. Students have rarely witnessed this model. For hundreds of years, the very nature of teaching has revolved around the teacher being in charge and the students having no power at all.

Generally, as soon as a teacher walks into a classroom, students sense that they are about to give up control for the next 50 minutes. It does not have to be this way.

By involving our students in the development of course policies, guidelines, and rules, we are creating a system of shared governance in which students take greater responsibility for their own actions and for the learning environment. Several years ago, a young faculty member sought my advice when he wanted to give his students some say in course policies, including attendance, tardiness, missed or late assignments, and cheating and academic misconduct. We decided together that he should use a simulation activity in which each student took on the role of the president of a small welding engineering company (engineering was his field). As president, each was to develop an employee handbook that outlined the company's policies concerning attendance, tardiness, incomplete or late work, and cheating or stealing from the company. Students were told that these policies would provide the framework for their course policies.

The result was that students recommended policies in which they had more accountability than they would have if the professor had developed the guidelines alone. The students indicated that their policy recommendations were a reflection of their beliefs about how employees should act in the workplace.

My young colleague was surprised by the outcome. He had feared that his students would get carried away and come up with guidelines designed simply to make their lives easier. He was delighted to see that they had a solid understanding of the roles and responsibilities required in the work world as well as the ability to transfer these ideas into a classroom setting. His experience as a student had led him to doubt that students were capable of acting maturely and responsibly regarding these matters. The simulation activity taught him that he could trust his students, he just had to give them the opportunity to show him they were worthy of his trust.

Engaging students in course policy and guideline discussions has an additional benefit beyond giving them a sense of ownership of their learning; it shifts the responsibility for enforcing these guidelines from the teacher to the entire student community. If a student is absent, late, or misses a test, he or she was directly involved in drafting the policies used to deal with these behaviors. We are no longer the sole creator or enforcer of rules. Sharing responsibility based on fairness and collective input greatly reduces the adversarial role between teacher and student. It also promotes increased responsibility among our students, leading to an improved learning environment for all involved.

When students are given the opportunity to act in mature and reasonable ways, they will rise to the occasion. Trust is empowering. The worst thing that can happen is that we'll need to work with students to consider the ramifications of their ideas if they fall outside of what is reasonable and will not optimize their learning. Learner-centered teaching is not without risks, but the risks involved are well worth taking.

Learning Tasks and Assignments

Choice should also be offered about what and how to learn. I am not suggesting that we turn the curriculum over to students but, rather, that we give students choices in situations where topics of inquiry are open. For example, if we are asking students to complete a writing assignment for which several books or articles would meet the requirements of the course, we should allow students to choose the topic that interests them. We all engage more readily when we are interested in what we are learning. However, there are other important reasons for giving students choices in what and how to learn.

When students are allowed to choose learning that interests them, they are more likely to develop a deep understanding of the material. This happens because their interest in the topic usually comes from already knowing something about it, or from personal curiosity.

Another reason for promoting student choice is that it encourages responsibility. When students choose a topic, they have no one to blame but themselves if they don't follow through on the assignment. Students can't complain that they were unmotivated by the topic without looking foolish. When students make learning choices, they are engaging in behavior that will serve them well in many other realms. Teaching students to make good choices is one of our most important responsibilities, regardless of subject area.

Assessments of Learning

If we are to optimize our students' opportunities to learn, we must allow them, when possible, to show us what they've learned in ways that are optimal for them. As we witnessed in the puppet show story recounted earlier, when we provide assessment options for our students, they will be able to use their learning strengths to demonstrate what they've learned. In the process, hidden talents and capacities might be revealed.

Helping Students Take Charge

Many aspects of our courses lend themselves to promoting student choice and allowing students to take more control of their learning experience. Several are explored below.

1. *Rewriting.* Rewriting is a common activity in composition classes but can be adapted for any course situation. Students can choose to rewrite papers for higher grades provided the initial effort meets some basic standard. Rewriting will improve the final product and help students develop metacognitive awareness by causing them to review the material and consider and use teacher feedback to determine what needs to be improved and what was already done well in the original work. Using feedback to improve work is another important lifelong learning skill, so the time and effort we put into providing feedback is time well spent.

2. *Retesting.* The same rationales hold true for giving students opportunities to retest to improve their learning. If our goal is for students to learn our course material deeply, then having them relearn the test material that was unclear or incomplete will help us achieve that goal. The test then becomes not just a message to students about what they knew or did not know, but a learning tool to deepen and improve their understanding of the course material. When we retest, we are allowing students who did not get it right the first time, to go back and figure out why it was wrong and fix the problem. Learning to fix what was wrong by identifying the gaps in their learning or problems with their test preparation is a very important metacognitive process. The message of retesting is that learning is what is important, not grades

3. *Choosing the Textbook.* Allowing students to review new textbooks being considered is another way to offer choices and facilitate students' learning. Much can be gained by soliciting student input when choosing a new text. Students are, after all, the ones who will be reading the books and the ones who have been reading them for the past

12–16 years. Students can tell us how user-friendly the book may or may not be. They can tell us if the reading level is appropriate, and if the ancillary material (CDs, study guides, online versions) is useful. When we combine their input with our needs and requirements, we will have a strong basis for making a good choice.

4. *Negotiating Deadlines and Test Dates.* A college class must have a structure and a timeline to accomplish its learning goals. However, within that structure, there may be room to give students choices about dates and deadlines. Allowing students to have a say about optimal deadlines and test dates gives them a genuine sense of control over two of the most important aspects of their course work. In many programs at Ferris State, faculty unwittingly end up giving their tests within a day or two of one another throughout the semester. This puts their students into crisis mode several times each semester. Sharing power over when tests are given or projects are due can prevent these crises from occurring and will give our students a better chance to show us what they know by having adequate time to prepare.

5. *Co-Developing the Criteria for Grading.* If we want our students to take more responsibility for their own learning, we have to put them in situations where they are asked to act responsibly. One such situation might be asking them to help develop the criteria for grading various aspects of the course work, including written work, presentations, and group work. This process will allow us to gain valuable insights into what students view as important aspects of learning and what they believe are fair criteria for assigning grades. We will be able to determine if our students really understand what makes a quality paper or an outstanding presentation. This information will tell us if we need to alter our expectations for the learning tasks we assign. In addition, by sharing the grading criteria with students, we reinforce our trust in them and motivate them to engage more fully in their learning process. We have given them a sense of control over the single most powerful aspect of the course (to them)—the grade.

6. *Setting Office Hours.* Perhaps the most visible sign of a learner-centered teacher is setting office hours at times that are most convenient for our students. To do this we will need to poll our classes about the times and days that work best for them and use this information to accommodate as many students as possible.

Helping Students Make Good Choices

> Destiny is not a matter of chance, it is a matter of choice; it is not a
> thing to be waited for, it is a thing to be achieved.
>
> —William Jennings Bryan

In making the case for sharing power with our students, I have neglected to address one important aspect of this process. What if the students don't want to make all of these choices or take more control of their learning? What if they see these actions as giving them more work and more responsibility, and they resist? What do we do? The answer is, we go slowly (Weimer, 2002, p. 29). Any new approach can make students uncomfortable when it falls outside their view of and expectations for school. However, we have human nature on our side in this process. It is the nature of the human brain to want to control what happens to it, to the greatest extent possible (Zull, 2002, p. 52). Researchers have proven that having choices in what and how to learn improves the motivation and engagement of students by letting them work on things they are interested in learning (Deci & Ryan, 1991; McCombs, 1991, 1994). We can increase students' desire to take control of their learning by creating learning environments that are safe and promote risk taking, and where mistakes are expected and accepted as a normal part of the learning process. As I mentioned earlier, UCLA psychologist Robert Bjork (1994) asks teachers, where do you want your students to make their mistakes? I would hope the answer is in the safety of our classrooms, with us there to guide them. When students realize the empowerment that comes from taking charge of their own learning, there will be no holding them back.

Skills to Make Effective Choices

There is much information available to help us teach our students to make good choices. I have reviewed much of it and have listed below a compilation of the most common suggestions.

1. Get students to consider as many options as possible; don't let them choose the first topic that pops into their mind.
2. Ask students to predict the outcomes of making a given choice. For example, they should ask themselves, "If I choose this topic, will I

find enough resources to do a good job?" or "Is the task manageable, and will I have enough time to complete it?"

3. When making a choice, consult with others. It is your choice, but others can help you consider issues you may have overlooked.

4. Teach students how to learn from mistakes. Teach them how to evaluate their choices after the fact to see what could have been done to improve the decision-making process and what went right about the choice.

5. Insist students take time to reflect on their options before pulling the trigger. This can help them avoid making silly mistakes.

Sometimes Choices Are Limited

For each of the areas of choice and control discussed in this chapter, the context of our own teaching will affect to what extent we can or cannot give students more choices and control over their learning. In a class of 200, the size alone limits some options, but not all. Choice and control lead to greater involvement and trust. There is no way to say we are optimizing our students' opportunities to learn and not work to give them as much control and as many choices as possible. It's just good teaching to do so.

8

WHEN STUDENTS TEACH
ONE ANOTHER

Teaching is the highest form of understanding.

—Aristotle

Tell me and I forget. Show me and I remember.
Involve me and I understand.

—Chinese proverb

In learner-centered classrooms, students regularly teach their peers. It is
our job to help them develop the basic skills and confidence to do this.
As teachers, we understand how much time, effort, and preparation goes
into teaching a lesson effectively, even when we know the content thoroughly. For students, this time, effort, and preparation will also include
learning the content or skills they will teach. Although our students have
watched teachers for thousands of hours, they have little familiarity with the
planning and delivery processes of teaching. If teaching others is to be a
meaningful learning experience, we must do an effective job of teaching our
students how to teach.

Rationales for Having Students Teach Each Other

When we ask our students to teach, we place them in a learning situation
that requires that the one doing the teaching thoroughly understands the
knowledge or skill set being taught. Having students teach one another promotes deep learning.

A second learning benefit that comes from asking students to teach is
that the student/teacher must consider how best to learn all he or she will

need to know about the assigned or chosen topic. The student/teacher will have to locate credible sources of information and mine those sources for the most important ideas, concepts, and facts to develop a full understanding of the topic. This may include consulting human resources, including librarians, and content experts on campus or around the world via the Internet. The student/teacher will also likely spend some face-to-face time with us as he or she develops a teaching plan. All of these actions represent important lifelong learning skills. Having students teach promotes independent learning and the willingness, ability, and confidence to accept increased responsibility for their own learning.

A third rationale for having students teach one another is that the students will gain an increased appreciation of the effort and skills required for effective teaching. They will have to confront issues such as how to get students involved in learning and what examples, stories, or analogies will best connect their topic to the background of their peers. Our students will, at the very least, have to reconsider what they think about the work teachers do every day to be ready to help them learn.

The final rationale for having students teach is the positive effect it will have on their public speaking skills. Students will be forced to communicate the material to their peers in a clear, concise, and meaningful manner. Students will be in front of their peers in a public environment that simulates the kind of professional setting many of them will experience in their future professions. Communication is one of the most important career and lifelong learning skills for our students to develop.

Helping Our Students Learn How to Teach

Step One: Choosing a Topic

Our individual course learning outcomes will determine whether to assign a topic to a student or group of students or to have the students choose a topic to teach. As I discussed earlier, giving students choices leads to increased responsibility and motivated, independent learning.

To ease students into teaching, we can assign narrow topics that will only take 5–10 minutes to teach, such as teaching the class how to do a specific type of problem in math or chemistry. When students are ready, particulary upperclassmen, the teaching assignment can be highly challenging, requiring significant effort and time to prepare, and requiring students to teach for an entire class period. All student teaching should be used to promote students' learning, and it should require more of students than just reporting the facts surrounding the topic. Cases or authentic problems from the course content are ideal teaching topics. Also effective is having students explain concepts or main ideas using images, analogies, and examples that help explain the material and its applications. These kinds of topics require students to explore sources beyond their textbooks. It will also require them to consult with us, giving us an opportunity to deepen their understanding and help prepare them for delivering the lesson.

Step Two: Understanding the Level of Content Expertise Needed to Teach a Topic to Others

One of the benefits that comes from having students teach is that they develop an understanding of the depth and breath of knowledge needed to teach material to others. This is especially meaningful, since most of their own learning has been on a "need to know basis," learning only what they need to know to earn a specific grade or pass a particular test. To be prepared to teach, our students will have to know not only the facts and vocabulary terms but also the whys and hows and uses of the topic they will teach.

When preparing students to teach, it is helpful to provide a list of questions that, when answered, will tell them they have a thorough understanding of a topic. Figure 8.1 contains a list of questions that will help students to judge their readiness.

Step Three: Deciding What the Class Should Know

All effective teaching begins with a statement of learning outcomes. For example, an outcome for a class, called Teaching Reading in the Content Areas, which I taught for many years, is described below.

> Students will by the end of the semester be able to demonstrate by classroom presentations and written reports how to facilitate students' learning using text material in a classroom setting to include: pre-reading techniques, a variety of reading guides, discussion techniques, question writing, cognitive mapping, vocabulary development and fix-up strategies.

All teachers know that a learning outcome is the basis for all lesson planning. This is the same for our student teachers. They must select what they want their peers to learn from all of the ideas, concepts, facts, vocabulary,

FIGURE 8.1
Do I Know the Topic Well Enough to Teach It to Others?

- How and where does this topic fit in the overall learning of this course?
- How many important parts, pieces, steps, subtopics, or main points make up this topic?
- Do you have a clear understanding of the important/technical vocabulary of this topic, and are you comfortable using it?
- Can you give clear examples that would allow others to more easily understand the topic?
- Can you write a clear explanation of the topic in your own words?
- Can you explain how the topic information is organized? What would others need to learn first, second, third, etc., to help them understand it fully?
- Can you find images that would clearly represent the ideas, concepts, actions, and uses of this topic?
- Can you explain how to use the topic (if applicable) to solve problems discussed in this course?
- Can you explain the most difficult aspect of understanding this topic?
- Do you feel you could answer most of the questions your peers might ask you about this topic?

---

and skills they possess about the topic. Making a list of learning outcomes is the first step in planning the teaching process.

Step Four: Organizing Material to Optimize Students' Learning

As our students prepare to teach, they must organize the information in a structure that is optimal for learning. They must consider whether their peers need any background information or introductory material to connect to the topic, and whether they need a brief review of other course material related to this topic before they introduce new material. Teachers must ask themselves these questions when trying to optimize their students' opportunities to learn.

The next step is to determine whether the information already has a structure or pattern built into it that naturally organizes it for learning. For example, is the information hierarchal or linear in nature? Is it part of a timeline, or does it already exist in a pattern-like comparison and contrast or similarity and difference format? These familiar patterns are easily recognized by learners and are ideal ways to organize information. If these patterns are not readily visible, then the students need to consider in what order the information and ideas should be introduced. This step-by-step process is continued until a meaningful and clear order has been organized.

There are no absolutes about how best to organize information for instruction, so students should be told to trust their own ideas about how the information will make the most sense to their peers. We can always check the order to make certain it has a reasonable structure before our students present it to the class.

Step Five: Choosing the Best Approach for Teaching the Topic

Our students will need our guidance as they plan the delivery of the information or skill(s) they will be teaching. Encouraging them to use their creativity and imagination should be an important part of our guidance. With the Internet as a resource, it is possible to have students research the various teaching methods and approaches before deciding on the best way to teach their peers. Keep in mind, however, that our students are most familiar with teacher-centered, lecture-centered learning, and it will require some courage and encouragement to get them to engage their peers in a more learner-centered format.

Here are some basic guidelines:

1. Whatever method student teachers choose, it must involve their peers in active learning—for example:

   > Playing a game
   > Working in pairs to solve problems
   > Going to the board to work on problems
   > Drawing a concept map of their understanding
   > Answering questions in pairs and sharing answers
   > Doing a role play

2. The delivery should include images that help illustrate and clarify the topic being taught.
3. The delivery should include examples, analogies, and/or metaphors that will aid in understanding the topic.
4. In most situations a handout should be distributed to reinforce the learning process—for example:

> Concept map of the topic
> PowerPoint slides
> Outline of the topic
> Set of key questions

5. There should be a beginning, middle, and end to teaching the topic.
6. The beginning is an introduction that establishes what is to be learned and attracts and motivates students—for example:

> A set of questions that will be answered by the end of the teaching
> A cartoon that illustrates some aspect of the learning
> A brainstorm session to see what everyone might already know about the topic
> A story that illustrates or builds a context for the topic

The middle should include not only information and facts, but also examples, images, discussion, activities, demonstrations, and practice (of a skill or problem process).

The end reviews and summarizes what was taught to reinforce the new learning. It can include a formative feedback activity such as "Tell me the two most important things you learned today" or "Tell me what is still not clear from today's class." Angelo and Cross's book *Classroom Assessment Techniques* (1993) is a great source for other appropriate formative feedback techniques.

Step Six: Understanding Teacher Responsibility

Perhaps one of the most important aspects of having students teach one another is that the students being taught understand they are just as responsible for knowing the material taught by their fellow students as they are for knowing the material we teach them. For this to be a true learning experience for everyone, students must be clear about this point. As many of us have discovered in our own teaching, when our classes include guest speakers, group presentations, or individual student performances, our students tend to see these learning opportunities as less important or even as days off. In a learner-centered classroom, students teaching each other, helping each other, and critiquing each other are all common events. We need to reinforce that our students will be held responsible for what they are asked to learn from one another, not just what they are asked to learn from us.

Whether we want to have our student teachers include an evaluation activity as part of their teaching plan will depend on our learning objective and the context of the course. Time constraints and the size of the class, among other issues, may determine whether to include an evaluation. In most cases, the student doing the teaching would be asked to provide an evaluation tool that we could adapt to test or assess the learning of the class. Some possible tools might include:

- Problem sets
- Short cases
- Essay questions
- Multiple-choice questions
- Summary writing
- Reflection journal questions

Step Seven: Giving Feedback to the Student Teacher

The last step of the student-as-teacher process is class feedback. As with all meaningful feedback activities, this one benefits both the receiver and the giver. Class members will be asked to give constructive feedback about their classroom experience, which will enable the student teacher to determine what was done well and where there is room for improvement. The student teacher must be open and receptive to this feedback and might be asked to write a brief report on how he or she will use the feedback to improve his or her future teaching. The act of giving and receiving feedback is a lifelong learning and career skill that students must develop. Providing the opportunity to practice this skill in our classrooms is extremely beneficial. Appendix C includes a rubric for the feedback process.

Conclusion

There is little debate that significant learning comes from teaching others. More than 40 years ago, the National Testing Laboratories (now the NTL Institute of Alexandria, Virginia) reported that retention of information after 24 hours was highest among those who taught the information to others. Even if there is not enough time in your course to have students teach a lesson, it would be incredibly valuable to ask them to prepare a topic for teaching. The thought and research process required to complete this assignment make it a powerful and effective learning tool, even if it doesn't include actually teaching the topic.

PRESENTATIONS AND PERFORMANCE ASSESSMENTS

The following six words can significantly improve the quality and depth of students' learning experiences:

Your work will be made public!

When we consider all the possible ways to optimize our students' learning, these six words rise to the top of the list. Preparing work for public consumption increases accountability. When students know their work will be made public, they become more serious and take more time and care in preparing it. Making work public also allows for assessment from additional audiences. When others see, hear, and evaluate students' work, an authentic, real-world model of how information is used, studied, and evaluated is created. When students enter the world of work, the influence or acceptance of their ideas, innovations, and solutions will depend on their presentation abilities. When they share their work with employers, colleagues, customers, clients, or board members, a common occurrence in the workplace, it must be presented in an accessible, concise, and persuasive manner. Our students must know how to present their ideas effectively to a wide range of audiences. Many will need help in developing the confidence and skills required to do this, and many will be quite unhappy about making their work public. Eventually, however, they will be thankful that we held them publicly accountable for the quality of their work, because this process develops and sharpens important skills that will serve them throughout their lives.

Thirty-three years ago I began my teaching career as a composition teacher. When I first began assigning papers for my students to write, I decided to have them read their papers aloud so each member of the class could see how his or her peers dealt with the same topic. My students protested loudly, however, and I relented and read the papers myself. On only a few occasions did I pick a very well-written paper and read it to the class. Looking back, relenting was one of many errors I have made in my teaching career. When students know their work will be displayed in public, whether it is on a course website or read aloud to their classmates, they put more effort and care into it. When students know that only the teacher will see their work, they may not put forth their best effort, since only one other person will see the result.

How Much Help Do Students Need?

Our students have been making presentations since their first "show and tell" in preschool or kindergarten. Most have been before an audience in school plays or when giving speeches. Most have taken a drama course, performed in recitals, participated in role-plays, or engaged in any number of other activities that have put them in front of people. However, most of these activities were not solo performances and did not include an audience that was there to critique the quality of the work presented. Most students will need serious encouragement and substantive skill development to become effective presenters.

Rationales for Using Presentations and Performance Assessment

Two outcomes are assessed with every presentation given: one is the presenter's skills in sharing the information with the audience, and the second is the quality of the information shared. The first rationale for using presentations as a learning tool is that effective presentations require presenters to know their material very well. Preparing and delivering presentations will drive students to engage with material more thoroughly, which will lead to deeper learning. Students must know not only the facts, but also the whys and hows of the information as well as its uses and applications. Presenters also need to be prepared for questions from the audience and ready to defend their answers or conclusions. All of these preparation activities lead to enhanced learning.

The second rationale for developing solid presentation skills is that they promote the enhancement of students' organization and communication skills. When preparing presentations, students must determine the most effective way to communicate their ideas to their audiences. They must consider what structure or pattern will make the information easiest for their audience to understand, and how to combine text and images to better communicate the material.

A third rationale is that presentations improve students' comfort levels with public speaking, even those who struggle with this process. Our classrooms should be one of the safest places to practice this very important career-enhancing skill. Presentations are an authentic expression of what our students will be asked to do in their future professions. Their ideas will be of little value to colleagues or employers if they are not shared in clear, organized, and effective ways. Our students will spend a significant portion of their work lives sharing information, and presentations are great practice for this.

Understanding How Presentations Promote Learning

Learning requires experience, but it also requires reflection, the ability to develop abstractions, and active testing of these abstractions (Zull, 2002, p. 18). When students are asked to present their findings, ideas, solutions, or conclusions, they are also being asked to test their abstractions by moving their ideas from the abstract inner world of their minds to the concrete outer world of the classroom. When they present, they open their ideas to the input, critique, and criticism of others. They find out whether their peers accept their ideas, whether others think like they do, and whether their thoughts and insights are clear to others. They also learn who disagrees and why, who has a different viewpoint, or who has another way of solving a problem. All of these outcomes enhance their metacognitive development.

Presentations and other forms of sharing ideas represent an important way for students to complete the learning cycle that arises naturally from the structure of the brain (Zull, 2002, p. 19). Active testing of ideas is where the rubber meets the road in learning. Learners make their ideas concrete (public) and find out if others think they make sense. Presentations deepen learning because they cause the learner to consider what, among all they have learned, is most important for others to hear, and how this information should be organized so it can be delivered meaningfully and clearly.

Encouraging Those Who Would Rather Not Present

Only the fear of snakes ranks higher than the fear of public speaking in public opinion polls. The fear of dying follows in third place. Yet almost every profession our students will enter requires solid public presentation skills to achieve success. When helping our students develop effective presentation skills, and overcome their fears and anxieties about speaking in front of people, we should focus on the emotions involved in public speaking. Our encouragement should focus on three areas:

1. helping students with their personal emotions related to presentation;
2. creating a positive and safe classroom environment where presenting is valued and supported; and
3. encouraging peer relationships that create support for taking the risk to speak in front of the class.

Helping With Personal Emotions

As is the case with other skill areas discussed in this book, there is an unlimited amount of easily accessible information that can help our students overcome their fears of presenting and learn to make effective presentations. Below are several suggestions from the literature on conquering the fear of public speaking and helping our students manage their emotions when speaking in front of others.

- Realize that most people feel like you do, so you are not alone, and you are most likely better at it than you think you are.
- Accept that this is a skill you will need for your professional life, so each experience is practice for the real world.
- Know your information very well. Confidence will come from knowing the material thoroughly and accurately.
- Practice your presentation in front of a mirror or in front of friends. Practice builds confidence.

- Take at least three deep breaths before you begin to speak. Deep breathing helps the body to relax.
- Distract yourself before beginning the presentation—keep your mind on something other than the presentation. This will help keep you relaxed.
- Have your notes (cards, PowerPoint slides, etc.) highlighted to indicate the points you want to stress so you can find them easily. Also, have the information printed in a large font so it is easy to see. Finally, number the cards or slides so if they get mixed up, you can easily put them back in order.

Creating a Positive Learning Environment

Creating a positive and safe classroom environment where presenting is valued and supported is key to making it an effective tool for student learning. Much has been written about the need to create emotionally safe learning environments as a way to encourage student risk taking (Bjork, 1994). One of the best ways to do this is to have students help develop a set of guidelines for the audience's behavior that promotes a supportive and thoughtful response. You can use the activity outlined in chapter 6 for setting guidelines for group work to develop audience response guidelines. These guidelines should also include appropriate ways to challenge, critique, or criticize the presenter's ideas or findings.

Most audiences want to hear what a presenter has to say. However, there will be times when not everyone is interested in students' presentations. Nonetheless, as our students work to develop effective presentation skills, we must create a classroom environment that supports each of them as they improve and develop these skills.

Encouraging Peer Relationships

It is ironic that the fear public speaking strikes in the hearts of many of our learners can actually be used to create the kind of supportive learning community we all would love to have in our classrooms. We can accomplish this by getting our students to understand that they are all in this presentation thing together. By establishing a kind of "Three Musketeers" attitude, our students will develop a genuine desire to support one another. After all, each and every one of them will be up in front of the class at some point during the semester. This kind of support is not created instantly; it must develop and grow over time. Indeed, some students will enter our classrooms believing that they should not have to take any responsibility for the learning success of their peers. We must help these students understand that working collectively and supporting one another is not only a way to improve presentation skills, it is also a vital career and lifelong learning skill they can't afford to ignore.

Getting Students Started

We can't expect our students to take on major presentations without practicing their burgeoning skills in smaller, more manageable exercises. I discuss several ideas below to help students get their feet wet.

Reporting Findings From Small-Group Work

One of the easiest ways to get students started with presentations is to have them report on small-group work by coming to the front of the room to share their findings. When forming groups, let students know that their findings will be made public, and that one member of the group will be asked to come to the front of the classroom and report. Tell them that any member of the group can be called on to present the findings, so each of them should be prepared to deliver the report, state the findings, and indicate, by name, which group members were responsible for each of the points, ideas, and solutions that are shared. This process increases the likelihood that students will engage substantively in the group work and be prepared to provide a meaningful and well-thought-out report. It also reduces the likelihood of groups having social loafers, those students who let others do the work but want the credit or grade the group as a whole earned.

Another option is to have the groups record their findings on transparencies (this is not needed if you have an ELMO or other document camera in the classroom), so the rest of the class can review their work visually.

Once the presentation is complete, open the floor to other students to question, disagree, or suggest alternatives to the presenter as a means of encouraging deeper engagement with the material, which will result in deeper learning.

Presenting Homework

Another way to help students build confidence in their presentation skills is to have them make short presentations about their homework. Ask them to show how they solved a problem in math or chemistry, have them give an analysis of their reading assignment, or suggest they recount the actions they took to find an answer to a case they were preparing. Students should know that any student in the classroom could be called on to present, so everyone needs to be prepared. Although this kind of presentation might only last five minutes, it is an excellent way to get students to take greater responsibility for their homework and to give them public speaking practice.

Presenting Predictions

One of my favorite ways to assist students in developing their presentation skills is to have them present their predictions as they relate to the various problems or issues being studied. By making a prediction, students can practice their synthesis thinking without the pressure of having to present a single right answer. This process also serves as an excellent formative assessment of their thinking skills and offers insights into how well they have learned the material used in making the prediction. This activity can also be done in writing or in small groups. If we are looking for ways to sharpen our students' presentation skills, presenting predictions is a simple and effective way to do so.

Building Toward a Professional Presentation

> There are always three presentations, for every one you actually gave. The one you practiced, the one you gave, and the one you wish you gave.
>
> —Dale Carnegie

During the past five years I have listened to well over 100 presentations at state and national conferences on teaching and learning issues. These presentations were conducted, in most cases, by teaching professionals with significant experience talking in front of student and faculty audiences. Despite this, many of the presentations, although sharing useful content, did not reflect the standards of high-quality presentations outlined in the literature on public speaking. This is not meant as a criticism of my colleagues, but rather a suggestion that if faculty with considerable speaking experience are not living up to professional speaking standards, then we must be sure to set expectations for student presentations that reflect students' limited experience as presenters. Our students should be encouraged and expected to advance their presentation skills, but this must be done in a way that takes their level of experience into consideration.

There are hundreds of excellent resources we can consult to find information to guide the development of our students' presentation skills. Some focus on the physical delivery of information, including speaking, eye contact, audience interaction, and movement. Others highlight the ability to create effective visual images for presentations using PowerPoint slides, pictures, graphs, and charts. Still others offer advice on gathering and organizing material in a way that will result in a cohesive and effective presentation. Below is a list of suggestions I have been sharing with students for years about the basics of delivering an effective presentation. Many of my colleagues have used these suggestions as well. The list is not meant to be comprehensive, but rather to serve as an accessible starter kit of ideas.

1. Know who your audience is.
   a. Age
   b. Interest in the topic
   c. Attention span
   d. Level of education
2. Render your audience benign.
   a. Do or say nothing that would turn your audience against you.
   b. Be careful in the areas of humor, sex, politics, and religion.
3. Use emotional tools whenever possible—the brain remembers emotional information more easily.
   a. Stories
   b. Pictures
   c. Songs
   d. Images
4. Do not turn your audience into note takers; have a handout of main points with room to write a few additional notes.
5. Make it very clear what the audience will learn as a result of the presentation.

    a. List main points as an image on a slide or transparency and include them in your handout.

    b. Conclude your presentation by reminding the audience what they learned.

6. Plan the best way to reinforce and illustrate what you want the audience to learn.

    a. Examples, analogies, and metaphors

    b. Pictures, diagrams, maps, and charts

7. Know the content of the presentation well enough that you can deliver it without notes; keep it concise, clear, and organized.

8. Time your presentation before delivering it.

9. If you are not totally confident in your knowledge of any part of the presentation, leave it out—don't put yourself in a position where you have to wing it.

10. If asked a question to which you don't know the answer, say, "I don't know. That's a good question, and I'll have to look into it."

11. Don't read your presentation—deliver it!

Choosing the Performance of Learning

This chapter, on the use of performance in the classroom, focuses mainly on its value as a learner-centered assessment tool. However, there is a growing acceptance that performance in the arts is not simply an expression of feelings, but that it is cognitive in nature, providing the tools of thought needed to improve understanding across academic subjects, and to bolster imaginative, creative thinking capacities that are rapidly becoming societal necessities (Chicago Arts Partnership in Education, 2001). Arts-based performance of learning can be a powerful and useful teaching and learning tool for learner-centered classrooms.

A powerful case can be made that performance learning is not limited to dance and music classes, that it has a place across the curriculum as an additional way to optimize our students' opportunities to learn (Burnaford, Aprill, & Weiss, 2001). The Chicago Public Schools, through the Chicago Arts Partnership in Education (CAPE) Program (2001), have successfully used performance arts in classrooms since the early 1990s. This might involve dancers collaborating in teaching mathematics, drama specialists and musicians teaming up with history teachers, or visual artists working with English-language educators. As we explore the different ways we can optimize our students' learning, we will be limiting our students and ourselves if we don't consider the ways in which arts-based performance can enhance students' learning across all of our disciplines.

Performance Assessments

Conceptions of good assessment are moving away from brief written tests that correlate with the target aptitudes and toward direct observation of complex performance and (Linn, Baker, & Dunbar, 1991). In this newer model of performance assessment, students are observed working on complex tasks or dealing with real-life problems [Raizen & Kaser, 1989]. Jon Mueller, professor of psychology and developer of the Authentic Assessment Toolbox—the 2004 Merlot Award winner, puts it this way:

> We can teach students how to *do* math, *do* history and *do* science, not just *know* them. Then, to assess what our students learned, we can ask students to perform tasks that replicate the challenges faced by those using mathematics, doing history or conducting scientific investigation. (2006)

Performance assessment has been part of public education since the late 1980s. As a result, many of our students have experienced performance assessments as part of their K–12 or college experiences. The reality is, however, that performance assessment has not been the primary way our students have been assessed. As a result, they are likely to be much more familiar and comfortable with traditional paper-and-pencil testing. It is important to help students understand that one of the main reasons we are using performance assessments is their ability to enhance students' learning choices. The remainder of this chapter offers rationales for their use, explanations of their design features, and examples of various kinds of performance assessments and how to evaluate them.

Why Performance Assessments?

Performance assessments provide an authentic measure of what students have learned. Authentic assessments expect students to complete a full array of tasks that mirror the priorities and challenges found in the best instructional activities, including research, writing, revising, discussion, providing an engaging oral analysis of a recent political event, or collaborating with others on a debate (Wiggins, 1990).

Evidence strongly suggests that performance assessments are one of the most valid ways to find out what students have learned because they ask students to demonstrate their knowledge (Office of Research Education, 1993). The Office of Technology Assessment of the U.S. Congress describes performance assessment as testing that requires a student to create an answer or a product that demonstrates his or her knowledge or skills. Inherent in this definition is the notion that the process itself is quite important, not merely the selection of answers, as is the case in traditional testing situations (Rudner & Boston, 1994). Performance assessments require that students actively develop their approaches to the task assigned under defined conditions, knowing that their work will be evaluated according to agreed-upon standards. This requirement distinguishes performance assessment from other forms of testing.

Students' Choices and Performance Assessment

Performance assessments provide an opportunity to offer choices to our students and enhance their control of the learning process. We can let them choose how they would like to demonstrate what they've learned. Examples include a written report, a speech, a project presentation, or an oral exam. As an alternative, we can let them choose the topic of the performance, rather than the kind of performance. Giving choices encourages students to take more responsibility for their learning. Performance assessments, by their very nature, allow for more student choice and greater control in determining what method is used to exhibit academic competence. Even when students cannot choose their own topics or formats, there is usually more than one acceptable route to constructing a product or performance (Mueller, 2006).

Students' Roles in Performance Assessments

Authentic assessments require students to be effective performers with acquired knowledge. Traditional tests tend to reveal only whether students can recognize, recall, or "plug in" what was learned out of context (Wiggins, 1990). The list below outlines the core elements of effective performance assessments and explains how students' roles and responsibilities are different in this model from those in more traditional assessment measures.

Features of Performance Assessments

- Students will be active participants, not passive selectors of the single right answer.
- Intended outcomes should be clearly identified to the students and should guide the design of a performance task. Students can be included in developing the outcomes.
- Students should be expected to demonstrate mastery of those intended outcomes when responding to all facets of the task. Mastery is different from traditional testing where a student can average his or her right and wrong answers to pass a test. Some students will see this as unfair because it does not fit within their view of the learning process.
- Students must demonstrate their ability to apply their knowledge and skills to reality-based situations and scenarios.
- A clear, logical set of performance-based activities that students are expected to follow should be evident.
- A clearly presented set of criteria (rubric) should be available to help judge the degree of proficiency in a student response (adapted from the Prince George's County Public Schools, 2006).

With regard to the last feature, which involves having a rubric or well-developed criteria for measuring performance, it must both define the attribute(s) being evaluated and develop a performance continuum (Stiggins, 1991). For example, one attribute in the evaluation of writing might be writing mechanics, defined as the extent to which the student uses proper grammar, punctuation, and spelling. As for the performance continuum, categories can range from high-quality, well-organized, good transitions with few errors, to low-quality work with so many errors that the paper is difficult to read and understand. If there is not a clear sense of the full dimensions of performance, ranging from poor or unacceptable to exemplary, teachers will not be able to teach students to perform at the highest levels, or help students to evaluate their own performance. Both of these outcomes are vital aspects of a learner-centered classroom.

FIGURE 9.1
Performance assessment options.

- Designing and carrying out experiments and reporting the findings
- Writing essays that require students to rethink, integrate, or apply information
- Collaborating with others to accomplish tasks
- Demonstrating competence in using a piece of equipment or a technique
- Building models in the physical world and in virtual space
- Developing, interpreting, and using maps
- Making collections
- Writing term papers, critiques, poems, or short stories
- Delivering speeches or oral presentations
- Playing musical instruments or singing
- Participating in oral examinations
- Developing portfolios
- Teaching others
- Marketing a product
- Designing a product
- Planning an event
- Solving problems
- Resolving cases

Examples of Performance Assessments Categories

Most of the examples in Figure 9.1 are not likely to be new to our students, but they may need our assistance in understanding our expected outcomes and how best to use these options to prepare for the assessment.

Developing Standards to Measure Learning

Having identified the kind of performance we want from our students, the next step is to develop the standards by which to judge the performance. Figure 9.2 provides a helpful list of how to construct a set of standards or a rubric to measure student performance. Involving students in the development of the rubric is a great learning task. Students can take responsibility for identifying the characteristics and criteria they believe are most important in performing the assigned task. This involvement leads to greater understanding of the criteria on which they will be evaluated. It also sends the message that there are no surprises or tricks. We want them to succeed and to know how they will be evaluated (Stix, 1997).

FIGURE 9.2
Building a performance rubric.

Complete the following steps:

1. Identify the overall performance or task to be assessed, and perform it yourself or imagine yourself performing it.
2. List the important aspects of the performance or product.
3. Try to limit the number of performance criteria, so they can all be observed during a pupil's performance.
4. If possible, have groups of teachers think through the important behaviors included in a task.
5. Express the performance criteria in terms of observable student behaviors or product characteristics.
6. Don't use ambiguous words that cloud the meaning of the performance criteria.
7. Arrange the performance criteria in the order in which they are likely to be observed. (Airasian 1991, p. 244)

Sample rubrics for evaluating students' performances are in Appendix D.

Practice Makes Perfect

I want to end this chapter by sharing an example of how teaching our students to make effective presentations can have significant career benefits. During the spring of 2006, the social sciences department on my campus was busy hiring a new geographer. As part of the interview process, each candidate was asked to teach a lesson of his or her choice. Through the Ferris grapevine, word reached me that the candidate who was hired had given the finest teaching presentation the department head had ever witnessed in his 30 some years in higher education. Since I work with all of the new faculty on our campus, I was anxious to meet our new geographer and find out to what she attributed her great presentation skills. Her answer was that her undergraduate college required each student to make public presentations of his or her work at least once in every single course the student took. She had made approximately 50 presentations as an undergraduate student, which had given her a significant advantage when it came to professional interviews. Equally important was that it had given her a head start on being an outstanding teacher as well.

10

BECOMING LIFELONG
LEARNERS

Unless you act like a student the rest of your life
while keeping your job going, you're going to be
hopelessly out of touch.
                              —John Kettle

L ifelong learning requires an active learning style involving self-assessment, risk taking, self-discovery, and the ability to deal behaviorally
with difficult situations, for example, situations requiring assertiveness, listening, conflict management, giving feedback, or delegation (Bigelow, 1996, p. 307).

One place to start a discussion with students about the need to become
lifelong learners (LLLs) would be with the findings of Marcia Baxter-
Magolda's study of the impact the undergraduate experience on intellectual
development. Baxter-Magolda (1992) found that only 2 of the 101 students
in her study reached the highest level of intellectual development (contextual
knowing) while undergraduates. Most students only progressed through the
second stage (transitional knowing) by graduation. The undergraduate experience got them started on the road to adult reasoning, but whether they
reach the highest level of adult intellectual development (contextual knowing) will depend on the continued development of their intellectual skills.
Baxter-Magolda makes it clear that her study was limited by the demographics of the Miami of Ohio students and warns us not to generalize her findings
to more diverse populations. However, it is clear that an undergraduate degree is just a starting point in a lifetime of learning and cannot begin to fully
prepare our students for life in a global community.

We are examples of lifelong learners! We can share with our students the
continual learning we do to improve our teaching and stay current in our

subject areas. We need to help them see that lifelong learning is a must for us, despite any degree or license we have that says we're qualified to teach forever. For example, as new research appears on the human brain and how it works, we must update our teaching practices to reflect these new learning theories. Our students need to see, through us, that continual learning is not unusual; it is the norm for any career in today's global economy.

One Industry's View of Lifelong Learning Skills

When I began thinking about helping students develop lifelong learning skills, I realized I had a treasure chest of information sitting right next to me at dinner every night. My wife Julie is the coordinator of hospitality programs at Ferris State, and for 20 years has been asking her Program Advisory Board members, who represent all facets of the hospitality industry, what skills her hospitality students should have to be successful in such a diverse industry. With her help, I reviewed the minutes from dozens of board meetings and identified the skills most often cited as vital if students are to move beyond their entry-level jobs and be successful. Figure 10.1 contains a list of some of these growth skills, which are highly representative of the lifelong learning skills all of our students will need.

An interesting point to note about this list is the absence of some of the skills students spend a great deal of time mastering in college, including note taking, memorization, test taking, and cramming.

As educational institutions consider the many ways they can better prepare their students for our ever-changing world, they would do well to spend time developing skills that are part of the Advisory Board list, as opposed to skills that are not on that list but are a usual part of our students' college experience.

Lifelong Learning and the Covert Curriculum

One way to encourage our students to develop lifelong learning skills is to be honest with them about the limitations of their academic courses to fully develop skills that will enable them to learn on their own for the rest of their lives. In his article, "The Covert Curriculum: The Lifelong Learning Skills You Can Learn in College," Drew Appleby says two distinct curricula exist

FIGURE 10.1
Hospitality industry key lifelong learning skills.

1. Must be able to read large amounts of information, determine what is important to the task at hand from the reading, and quickly summarize it for others.
2. Must be able to learn on your feet from others—be able to observe and listen to others and quickly apply what was learned to your own work.
3. Must know the difference between the information you need to know and all the other information that is out there. In other words, you need to know what you don't know.
4. Must be able to learn from your mistakes, or you will be out of business.
5. Must be able to communicate clearly and concisely—to teach others so they understand and can apply what you have taught them.
6. Must have the skills to work and learn on your own; if given a task or assignment, you must know how to find the information you need to carry it out.
7. Must know your strengths and your weaknesses; otherwise you risk making bad decisions about which jobs you can do and which ones you will have to ask for help with.
8. Must be able to use a computer in a wide variety of ways and know how to learn new applications as they become available.
9. Must know how to plan and organize your own time and that of others very well.
10. Must know yourself well. Your values, morals, and ethics will be tested constantly.

within a college student's undergraduate experience. One is the more obvious "overt curriculum," made up of the list of classes on a transcript and the knowledge and skills learned in these classes (facts, concepts, and theories). The less obvious one is the "covert curriculum," composed of the skills and characteristics a student develops as a result of completing the overt curriculum (2001, p. 28). The covert curriculum is the one that produces lifelong learning skills. The extent to which our students acquire these lifelong learning skills has to do with how much they are willing to invest in their own human capital development (Shaffer, 1997).

Students who understand the importance of building up their human capital seek out academic experiences that foster the development of these covert skills, which include leadership, planning, public speaking, problem solving, getting along with others, and learning to learn. Students who limit themselves to the material in the overt curriculum are behaving as if future success depends solely on the ability to maintain a decent grade point average and learn the facts, concepts, and theories presented in their classes (Shaffer, 1997, p. 6).

Why Become a Lifelong Learner?

Every college student knows that being successful in his or her life's work will require more than just note-taking and test-taking skills. Despite this awareness, our students need to be reminded constantly that college is not the end of their learning but a preparatory process for a life of continual learning. One rationale to help students understand the need to be lifelong learners is the fact that the U.S. Department of Labor (2006) estimates people between the ages of 18 and 38 will change employers or occupations while working for the same employer 10 times. This statistic reinforces the fact that learning the content of college courses, while important, must be supplemented with the ability to learn new content and new skills throughout life. More important, students must recognize that the skills they will need most, no matter what their job, are likely the lifelong learning skills included in figure 10.1.

When *Apollo 13* was lost in space, computers figured out, in 90 minutes, how to bring it back. It's reported that it would have taken a scientist working with pencil and paper over a million years to figure out how to perform the same task. Eighty percent of all the scientists who have ever lived are alive today; their collective work adds 2,000 pages to man's scientific knowledge every minute, and the scientific material they produce every 24 hours would take one person 5 years to read. Approximately a half-million new books are published every year (countdown.org). I include these facts not because I wanted you to know how happy the *Apollo* astronauts were that humans had invented computers (although I suspect they were very happy), but as a way of framing a second rationale for lifelong learning.

The speed at which human knowledge is growing is so great that our students will have no choice but to see their lives as an endless learning experience if they are to stay competitive and employed. The "half-life of knowledge" is the time from when knowledge is gained to when it becomes obsolete. Half of what is known today was not known 10 years ago. In fact, the amount of knowledge in the world has doubled in the past 10 years and is doubling every 18 months, according to the American Society of Training and Documentation (Seimens, 2004, p. 1).

Our students need to manage their skills development as well as their skills application; they need to maintain a skills portfolio much like they do a resume (Evers, Rush & Berdrow, 1998).

Helping Students Become Lifelong Learners

It is our job as teachers to help our students acquire the skills they need to be lifelong learners. The three steps outlined below will aid this process.

Step One: Understanding the Purpose of College Has Changed

In a perfect universe, our incredible ability to teach and guide our students would result in graduating learners who no longer need teachers to learn because they are equipped with learning skills and strategies that allow them to tackle any learning task successfully. Of course, we don't live in a perfect universe, so a more modest and realistic goal might be to help our students understand that the assignments, activities, and assessments in our courses have been purposely designed to enhance their skills for lifelong learning and simultaneously teach course content. Students must understand that the roles and responsibilities of colleges have changed. In addition to teaching important knowledge and skills needed for immediate use, faculty must prepare students for a life of finding and producing new knowledge. With these new roles and responsibilities for colleges come corresponding new roles and responsibilities for students. Despite their long-held views of what school is supposed to be, students must now recognize that college is just one step in a lifetime of learning.

Step Two: Developing the Right Attitude

In Phillip Whitford's (1995) article, "The Five Most Important Life-Long Job Search Skills," the second skill the author identifies is *conscious learning*. By this he means that lifelong learning is more an attitude than an action. Lifelong learners are continually looking for ways to gain knowledge and skills, not just when they have a specific need for them, but because learning is what they value and learning is what learners do. Those who engage in conscious learning will have more to offer when opportunity knocks.

Step Three: Learning How to Learn Best

Being a lifelong learner has taught me that I have a very poor spatial sense. I didn't know this when I was in school, although receiving an F + in geometry should have been a strong indicator (bless you, Sister Rose Gerard). I didn't really recognize that I was challenged in this area until well after I was married and regularly turned seemingly easy home repairs into costly "call the professional" projects. My academic and home life would have been greatly enhanced had I known how very bad my spatial sense was. If our students are to be effective lifelong learners, it is vital that they know how they learn best and in what areas they are challenged. By helping students discover their strengths and preferences as learners, we can teach them how to "play to their strengths" as lifelong learners. Howard Gardner, who developed the theory of multiple intelligences (see figure 10.2), said that most employers would be thrilled to hire a person who excelled in just one of the eight areas he identified. Our students need our help in recognizing where their talents lie and our encouragement to follow where those talents lead them. Howard Gardner first introduced his theory of eight different kinds of intelligence in *Frames of Mind* (1993).

Today, students can determine their strengths and weaknesses with the click of a mouse. Dozens of quality websites include learning style inventories, multiple intelligences questionnaires, and study and learning skills surveys, but the best places for students to investigate these learning preferences are the career counseling services and academic skills or tutoring centers on their college campuses. As teachers, we can continually give students feedback as we discover their talents, strengths, and weaknesses.

FIGURE 10.2
Eight multiple intelligences.

- Linguistic intelligence: word smart
- Logical
- Musical intelligence: music smart
- Spatial intelligence: picture smart
- Bodily-kinesthetic intelligence: body smart
- Interpersonal intelligence: people smart
- Intrapersonal intelligence: self smart
- Naturalist intelligence: nature smart (Armstrong, 1994)

Developing Metacognitive Skills

Metacognition, an important concept in cognitive theory, consists of two basic processes occurring simultaneously: monitoring your progress as you learn, and making changes and adapting your strategies if you perceive you are not doing well (Winn & Snyder, 1996). Metacognitive skills include taking conscious control of learning, planning and selecting strategies, monitoring the progress of learning, correcting errors, analyzing the effectiveness of learning strategies, and changing learning behaviors and strategies when necessary (Ridley, Schultz, Glanz, & Weinstein, 1992).

Among all of the important skills our students need to be lifelong learners, metacognitive skills are perhaps the most important. Their importance becomes incredibly clear when comparing novice learners to expert ones. Novice learners are less likely to evaluate their comprehension, examine the quality of their work, or stop to make revisions as they go along. They are often satisfied with just scratching the surface of their learning. Novice learners don't attempt to examine a problem in-depth and often fail to make connections or see the relevance of the material to their lives. Expert learners however, who possess well-developed metacognitive skills, do all of the things the novices fail to do. They are "more aware than novices of when they need to check for errors, why they fail to comprehend, and how they need to redirect their efforts" (Ertmer & Newby, 1998).

A simple example of metacognition at work in reading is when a skilled reader comes across something in the text he or she does not understand and immediately determines the best way to deal with the problem. The reader will likely identify several alternatives, including continuing to read, hoping that the next paragraph will shed some light on the problem material; re-read the material, hoping to find a cue he or she missed; stop and look up the meaning of unknown words; or ask another person. All of these corrective strategies are part of metacognitive abilities. These readers are monitoring their reading comprehension, know when they have not understood, and take appropriate action. In my years of teaching developmental reading, many of my students' only strategy when they did not understand what they read was to close the book and turn on the TV.

To become effective lifelong learners, our students need to understand the learning strategies available to them as well as the purposes of these strategies. They also must develop the ability to select, use, monitor, and evaluate their use of these strategies. Metacognitive skills work best when they are learned well and can operate automatically (Vockell, 2004).

Figure 10.3 includes a list of activities that can be incorporated into our teaching process to build our students' metacognitive skills, an extremely important step in helping them to become lifelong learners.

The Big Four: Teaching the Four Key Skills for Lifelong Learning

In *The Bases of Competence: Skills for Lifelong Learning and Employability* Frederick Evers, James Rush, and Iris Berdrow (1998) address the continuing disparity between the skills developed in college and the essential skills needed in the dynamic workplace environment. Drawing on more than a decade of research on companies, graduates, and students, the authors identify four distinct skill combinations most desired by employers: managing self, communicating, managing people and tasks, and mobilizing innovation and change. These "Big Four" skills, as the authors describe them, are key elements in the development of effective lifelong learning abilities.

Learning to Manage Oneself

If our students are to be effective lifelong learners, one of the first skills they must develop is the ability to manage their own lives effectively. Self-management includes five key actions.

1. learning to take responsibility for one's own performance;
2. taking responsibility for developing the skills and competences needed to be effective lifelong learners;
3. learning to control one's behavior;
4. demonstrating the ability to improve one's performance; and
5. learning how to handle and adapt to changing, ambiguous, and often conflicting circumstances. (Evers et al., 1998, p. 54)

All of these important actions can be facilitated in a learner-centered environment by increasing the responsibilities we give our students for their own learning, and by increasing the choices we give them as a way of letting them take more control over their learning. For example, we can have students demonstrate how they used the feedback they received on a writing

FIGURE 10.3
Suggestions for building metacognition.

1. When learners succeed at tasks of any kind, focus their attention on and label the thinking skills that have enabled them to be successful.

2. Encourage students to reflect on what they do that is effective and to give names to these processes.

3. Model strategies by thinking aloud or by asking students why you did something when you successfully use a thinking skill yourself.

4. Encourage students to talk to themselves while they think. At early stages, it may be necessary for them to talk out loud, but eventually they should be able to talk silently to themselves about what they are doing.

5. Help students over-learn basic skills so they can afford the leisure to focus on how they are thinking rather than being overwhelmed by the basic skills needed for the task at hand.

6. Recognize the conditional nature of many thinking skills. Help students realize that a major part of using these skills is knowing *when* (not just *how*) to use them.

7. To encourage transfer, emphasize connections within and beyond the topic of a given lesson. Encourage integration of knowledge acquired on different occasions.

8. Provide feedback on the degree to which learners have evaluated their comprehension correctly, not just on the degree to which they have comprehended correctly.

9. Emphasize not only knowledge about strategies, but also *why* these strategies are valuable and how to use them.

10. Be aware that students may not transfer thinking strategies far from the original setting unless they are guided to do so.

11. Supply prompts to aid learners in monitoring the methods and depth at which they are processing information. These prompts can range from simple reminders or checklists to detailed, scaffolded instruction programs.

12. Avoid excessive dependence on external prompting. Although prompts may be necessary in early stages of the development of thinking skills, the ultimate goal is self-regulation.

13. Focus on affective or personality aspects as well as the cognitive components of thinking skills.

14. Encourage students to work together on higher-order activities, so they can model thinking skills to one another and evaluate the comparative effectiveness of various thinking strategies. For example, encourage them to ask one another why they employed certain cognitive strategies. (Vockell, 2004)

assignment (from teachers or peers) to improve their next writing assignment. Using feedback to upgrade their writing demonstrates that they are capable of improving their performance, one of the key lifelong learning actions listed above.

Another way to help students develop these important abilities is to remind them that employers expect a high level of initiative and self-development. Waiting to be told you should learn the newest knowledge or skill will not cut it in a global environment.

Developing Communication Skills

For students to be competent communicators, they must be clear about the message they are trying to send, be conscious of the identity of the appropriate audience, and know the most effective way to convey the message (Evers et al., 1998, p. 76). It goes without saying that communication skills are a big part of being a lifelong learner. Working to improve these skills can only benefit our students' personal and professional lives. The ability to communicate effectively was one of several of the skills identified by the Hospitality Advisory Board (see figure 10.1) as necessary for success beyond an entry-level position. I discussed the importance of oral and written communication earlier, as well as the need to help our students develop these skills, which will become a crucial part of their lifelong learning repertoire (chapter 5). One additional area our students need help in recognizing is how the written and oral language they use defines them in ways that go beyond their intended message. For example, some words that are acceptable in popular culture may be less acceptable in the more formal world of business, health care, or education. Using this kind of language may result in unforeseen consequences. Helping students recognize how others may react to, or make personal judgments based on, their language is a great contribution to their understanding of adult communication.

Managing People and Tasks

> Businesses are made by people. We've proven time and time again that you can have a wonderful shop, and put a bloke in there who's no good, and he'll stuff it up. Put a good bloke in, and it just turns around like that.
>
> —Gerry Harvey (n.d.)

Managing people goes beyond supervising attendance, punctuality, conduct, and efficiency. To get people to achieve at a high level, the person managing them must have commitment, goal orientation, alignment of purpose, perception of fairness and justice, and motivation (Evers et al., 1998, p. 94). Our students don't get many opportunities to manage people or tasks in a teacher-centered environment. However, in a learner-centered classroom, the opposite is true. For example, by rotating leadership positions in group projects, or small- and large-group discussions, every student can have the opportunity to manage both people and tasks. By having students make choices about their learning or develop and plan a lesson to teach, we are helping them to develop the skills needed to manage people and tasks. The five skills that are most important to managing people and tasks include:

1. coordinating;
2. decision making;
3. leading and influencing;
4. managing conflicts; and
5. planning and organizing.

Facilitating the development of these skills requires only a desire to include them when planning our instructional activities. An example of one way to include them would be to discuss with students ways to resolve conflicts in their small groups. When conflicts do occur, we should then let the students solve the problems themselves using suggestions from the discussion. By teaching the skills of conflict resolution first, and then staying out of the resolution process, we give students a genuine opportunity to discover one of the crucial skills needed to manage people.

Mobilizing Innovation and Change

Mobilizing innovation and change is the ability to conceptualize and initiate novel methods and ideas in the absence of complete information about risk and outcome (Evers et al., 1998, p. 19). Skills, including the ability to motivate change in the way people think, behave, and act, would be part of the skill set for mobilizing change. One way to facilitate the fourth of the "Big Four" lifelong learning skills is to provide our students with opportunities to deal with problems that do not have set answers and require application of information learned in another context. We should give students the chance to reconceptualize their roles, and the roles of others as they have been traditionally played out, as a way of developing novel solutions to real problems

(p. 19). For example, we can ask students who have a very fixed mind-set about their ability to learn math—real math haters—to take on the role of someone who struggles with math but will do whatever it takes to pass. Ask them to develop a list of things they can do to overcome being math-challenged, to describe what attitude they must have to succeed, and explain why taking these actions will result in passing math.

This exercise illuminates for students what it takes to change a fixed mind-set, and what's involved in getting people to consider changing their minds. Another way to help students develop their abilities to mobilize change is to create opportunities for them to find solutions to problems without fear of errors or concern that failure will be held against them. I have often wondered what my class would be like if I insisted that a student would get an A only if he or she took intellectual risks regularly. My guess is that I would have a much more engaged class, where greater learning takes place.

Lifelong Learning Is Always on Display

Lifelong learning skills are easily embedded into our daily learning activities and assignments. By being learner-centered teachers, we continually create learning opportunities that help develop the skills our students will need to be effective lifelong learners. We only need to point them out and reinforce their importance.

11

HELPING STUDENTS RECOGNIZE WHAT THEY KNOW, DON'T KNOW, AND MISUNDERSTAND

O ur students come to college with a range of prior knowledge, skills, beliefs, and concepts that significantly influence what they notice about the environment and how they organize and interpret it. This, in turn, affects their abilities to remember, reason, solve problems, and acquire new knowledge (Bransford et al., 2000, p. 10). To be effective teachers, we must know what our students know and don't know and what knowledge is misunderstood or incomplete. To be effective learners, our students must also know these things about themselves. The following story illustrates the problem all teachers face in dealing with the preconceptions our students have and how these preconceptions significantly influence what students notice about the environment and how they organize and interpret it (Confrey, 1990; Mestre, 2001).

> *Fish Is Fish* [Lionni, 1970] is a story about a fish who is keenly interested in learning about what happens on land, but cannot explore the land because of his breathing limitations. In the story he befriends a tadpole who grows into a frog and then sets out to explore the land and report back to him. The frog reports he saw all kinds of things like birds, cows, and people. In the book we see the fish's interpretation of what the frog told him in the form of a fish adapting to fit the new information he received. For example, the people were imagined to be fish who walked on their tails and the birds were fish with wings. (Bransford, et al., 2000, p. 11)

We know from the constructivist theory of learning that people construct new knowledge and understandings based on what they already know and believe (Cobb, 1994; Vygotsky, 1978). A logical extension of this theory is that we must pay attention to the incomplete understandings, false beliefs, and naïve renditions of concepts that our learners bring with them to any given subject (Bransford et al., 2000, p. 10). If we fail to address our students' background knowledge, the understandings they develop (just like the fish in the story) can be very different from what we intend. Abraham Maslow (2004) once said, "I suppose it is tempting, if the only tool you have is a hammer, to treat every problem as if it were a nail" (p. 15). We need to know what tools are in our students' tool boxes and help them become aware of when and where to use them and what additional tools they need to improve their learning practice. If the only learning tool our students have is memorization, then everything we teach them will likely be seen as something to be memorized. It is not that we don't want them to form long-term memories; we just want them to understand that unless those memories can be used to solve problems, create new knowledge, and are transferable to aid learning in new situations, the memories are of little use unless the student competes on *Jeopardy*.

Using Student Background Questionnaires to Gather Knowledge

There is clear evidence that learning is enhanced when teachers pay attention to the knowledge and beliefs learners bring to a learning task and use this information as a starting point for new instruction (Bransford et al., 2000, p. 11). To optimize learning in a learner-centered environment, we must discover what our students are bringing to the learning table. The first step in this process is to develop a student background questionnaire, which should be completed at the beginning of every course. The questionnaire can be designed to elicit a wide variety of student information, including subject matter knowledge, learning skills competence, learning preferences, computer skills, and general demographic information. All of this knowledge can improve our ability to facilitate our students' learning.

A sample of a background questionnaire developed by the fall 2006 faculty learning community at Ferris State is in appendix E. The questions represent what these faculty members thought would be helpful for them to know as they began teaching their students. It can be adapted to meet differing needs. Many faculty, when designing a background questionnaire, choose to include specific questions about course subject matter to give them a clearer sense of what their students know about the subject when they begin the course. Learning research strongly supports gathering as much information about a student's knowledge as possible as a way to aid teachers in making successful connections to students' prior knowledge and in managing the learning process. Teachers should give the rationale for the questionnaire before students are asked to complete it. Students should also be told that if they are uncomfortable with any question, they can simply skip it.

Recognizing the Benefits and Disadvantages of Preexisting Ideas

Even when we think we have done an excellent job of teaching a lesson, and we delivered the information in a highly organized and clear manner, our students' preexisting ideas still may have prevented them from accepting the new information or cause them to alter the information to fit their view. To really know that our students understood and accepted what we intended, it is necessary to do a great deal of checking.

Numerous research experiments demonstrate the persistence of preexisting understandings among college-age and older students, even after new models have been taught that contradict these naïve views (Bransford et al., 2000, p. 16). A traditional way to check students' understanding has been to give a test every few weeks and use the grades as indicators of their comprehension. This system does little to determine if a student's preexisting understanding has interfered with his or her learning. A preferable approach is to ask students regularly to tell us what they have learned in their own words, using examples and analogies that demonstrate their accurate understanding of the new material. Even our brightest students filter the new course material through their prior knowledge, and if they have misconceptions or incomplete existing knowledge, they are likely to arrive at conclusions different from what we intend. If we don't check, we won't know. In some cases, even when we check our students' understandings, their preexisting ideas are so ingrained that they are unwilling to give them up.

Several years back, while teaching a freshman seminar course, I was discussing the idea of an internal locus of control. I suggested that this mindset could allow someone to choose not to get upset even when provoked. I explained that it is possible to make choices about how we act, regardless of the external pressures we might feel. One of my students became very agitated and told me I was wrong. He said that if I wanted to make him mad, I could do it, and there was nothing he could do to prevent it. No matter how much I explained to him that his view was incorrect, and that research confirms that individuals can make choices to prevent them from getting upset, he refused to believe it. I was unable to alter this student's preexisting belief about the power external forces had on him, no matter how hard I tried.

On another occasion, one of our public administration faculty invited our local state senator to class to discuss how the real world of politics operated, deals were negotiated, and compromise was fashioned. After the presentation, several students told the faculty member that they did not believe the senator. They strongly believed that there was no way elected officials would make deals in the way the senator described.

I share these stories because they are rich examples of the need to check constantly to see how students are interpreting the new material we teach, and to recognize that some of their preexisting beliefs and misconceptions are powerfully held. In 1998, Operation Physics, an educational outreach of the American Institute of Physics identified 268 basic misconceptions of students as old as age 14 about various areas of science. These ranged from believing that the earth is the center of the solar system to questioning why, if energy is conserved, why are we running out of it. (Operation Physics, American Institute of Physics, 1998).

I've had more than one college physics professor tell me that, when students were asked to explain what would happen when a cannonball was fired into the air, they responded that it would go straight up and straight down—just like it does in Road Runner cartoons. For scientific understanding to replace naïve understanding, students must first reveal the latter and then be taught to see where it falls short (Bransford et al., 2000, p. 16).

Using Formative Feedback to Make Learning Transparent

Our students are not empty vessels waiting to be filled with knowledge. If they were, our tasks as teachers would be much easier. Instead, we must create activities and conditions that allow us to see and understand the preexisting ideas our students bring with them to our classrooms. Once their thinking is revealed, we will have a foundation on which we can help them build a more advanced understanding of the subject matter. The use of frequent formative assessments (assessments in which students receive specific feedback on their errors) is an effective way to make our students' preexisting ideas visible to them, to their peers, and to us (Angelo & Cross, 1993). Formative feedback helps learners become aware of any gaps that exist between their desired goal and their current knowledge, understanding, and skills. This feedback will also guide them through a process that is necessary to obtain a more complete understanding of the subject at hand (Ramaprasad, 1983; Sadler, 1989). The most helpful type of feedback provides specific comments about errors, specific suggestions for improvement, and encouragement to students to focus their attention thoughtfully on the task, rather than simply being concerned with getting the right answer (Bangert-Drowns, Kulick, & Morgan, 1991; Elawar & Corno, 1985). This feedback can be particularly helpful to lower-achieving students, because it emphasizes that improvement is a result of effort, rather than a fixed mind-set or lack of innate ability.

Black and Wiliam concluded from a meta-analysis of over 250 studies that efforts to strengthen formative assessment produced more significant learning gains for low-achieving students, including students with learning disabilities, than it did for other students (1998).

Are Students Using the Feedback?

Over lunch at a teaching and learning conference, I learned one of the most valuable lessons of my teaching career. An educator at my table was discussing a small study by the composition teachers at his university to determine what students did with the written comments they received on their returned papers. The study revealed that 50% of the students did not even read the comments; they just looked at the grade. The other 50% read the comments but did not use the information to improve their next composition. The conclusion was that the comments were a waste of faculty's time, and that changes needed to be made to make students use the feedback to improve their writing. The composition faculty decided they would begin requiring the students to write a summary of the comments that included an explana-tion of how they would use them to improve their next paper. When the students knew that the faculty would be looking for measurable improve-ments in their future writing, based on the comments the students received on the first assignment, the students took more responsibility for improving their writing. This luncheon discussion should serve as a caution: don't as-sume your students are using the feedback you give them. Asking students to acknowledge and use feedback also provides you with a practical way to check whether the time and effort we put into comments and feedback is well spent.

Are Students Learning?

Simple classroom activities, such as questioning and discussion, are easy ways to check what our students know and don't know about the new informa-tion introduced in class. These activities also provide an ideal opportunity to give feedback on the accuracy or completeness of their thinking. To involve the whole class, I suggest the following strategies:

- Invite students to discuss their thinking about a question or topic in pairs or small groups, and then ask a representative to share these stu-dents' thinking with the larger group (sometimes called think-pair-share).
- Present several possible answers to a question, then ask students to vote on them.
- Ask all students to write down an answer and the thinking steps or process they used to arrive at the answer. Read a few of them aloud.
- Have students write their understanding of vocabulary or concepts before and after instruction.
- Ask students to summarize the main ideas they've taken away from a lecture, discussion, or assigned reading.
- Have students complete a few problems or questions at the end of instruction and check their answers.
- Interview students individually or in groups about their thinking as they solve problems (Black & Wiliam, 1998).

Helping Students to Unlearn

> A responsible person must learn to unlearn what he has learned. A responsible person must have the courage to rethink and change his thoughts. Of course there must be good and sufficient reason for unlearning what he has learned and for recasting his thoughts. There can be no finality in rethinking.
>
> —Ambedkar, 1955

Of all of the issues discussed in this chapter, the most difficult to do is to help students "unlearn" ideas and concepts they originally believed to be true but are incorrect or incomplete. As a person who has taught many of my friends and family the game of golf (not always with great success), I have often found it easier to work with someone who was brand new to the game than someone who already had bad habits ingrained in his or her swing. Years of muscle memories for the wrong swing are difficult to overcome and require a great deal of practice and hard work to do so. Our students can also have years of memories for ideas that are wrong or misguided. If we are to optimize their learning, we need to identify these ideas and misconceptions and work with students to overcome them. Keep in mind that it will take time and practice on their part to be successful. Additionally, these old ideas and beliefs will never be completely unlearned. Like a bad golf swing that comes back at the worst possible time, our students' old learning can return if the new learning is not practiced enough to replace it.

12

STUDENT EVALUATIONS— THEMSELVES, OTHERS, AND THE TEACHER

Friend to Groucho Marx: "Life is difficult!"
Marx to Friend: "Compared to what?"

The only man who behaves sensibly is my tailor;
he takes my measurements anew every time he
sees me, while all the rest go on with their old
measurements and expect me to fit them.

—George Bernard Shaw

I love golf! What I love, in addition to its ability to teach patience, discipline, temper control (still working on that), and concentration, is that golf is a game of instant feedback. Each time I hit a golf shot, I know instantly if it was great, average, or poor. I don't have to ask anyone else to evaluate my golf shot—golf is self-evaluation at its best. I may not always know exactly what I did wrong (or right for that matter), but the instant feedback gives me the information I need to decide if I should ask others for help or I can figure it out for myself.

Golf is a great metaphor for what we want our students to do with their academic work. We want students to advance to a place where they can recognize if what they did was great, average, or poor. We want them to use that information to seek out appropriate help or recognize that they can fix their errors themselves. How do we help our students reach this point of self-awareness? This chapter explores a body of research that focuses on teaching students how to self-evaluate. This chapter also looks at helping students to evaluate the work of others, and teaching them to give us meaningful feed-back so we can improve our ability to help them learn.

What Is Student Self-Evaluation?

Self-evaluation is defined as students judging the quality of their work, based on evidence and explicit criteria, to do better work in the future (Rolheiser & Ross, 2000). When we teach students how to assess their own progress, and they do so against known and challenging quality standards, a great deal of learning can take place. Self-evaluation is a potentially powerful technique because of its impact on student performance through enhanced self-efficacy and increased intrinsic motivation. Perhaps just as important, students like to evaluate their work (p. 1). Evidence of the positive effect of self-evaluation on student performance is particularly convincing for difficult tasks (Arter, 1994; Maehr & Stallings, 1972), and among high-needs pupils (Henry, 1994).

In their summary of the self-evaluation literature, Rolheiser and Ross (2000) report that research proves that self-evaluation plays a key role in fostering an upward cycle of learning. When the results of students' self-evaluations show their work to be of high quality, this awareness encourages students to set higher goals and commit more personal resources and effort to achieving them. This combination of goals and effort equals achievement.

Teaching Self-Evaluation

When we give students a rubric or a set of criteria to use in judging their work, we are often baffled that, despite these clear and specific directions, their final work is incomplete or poorly done. What students are likely missing is a clear understanding of how to use the rubric to self-evaluate; they need us to model the self-evaluation process. In the next few pages, I use the assignment of writing a persuasive essay to illustrate how we can help our students learn to self-evaluate. I use the four-stage process developed by Rolheiser and Ross (2000) as a guide.

The process begins by defining self-evaluation. As described earlier in this chapter, self-evaluation is when students judge the quality of their work, based on evidence and explicit criteria, to do better work in the future. The two key concepts students need to understand are "evidence" and "explicit criteria." What evidence would suggest that an essay is persuasive, and what are fair criteria to judge good writing?

Four Stages to Teaching Self-Evaluation

As described by Rolheiser and Ross (2000), there are four stages to follow when teaching students to self-evaluate. These stages are discussed below.

Stage One

In the first stage, we must involve students in *defining the criteria* that will be used to judge their essay. This can be done through large-group brainstorming, small-group discussion, or asking each student individually to make a list of suggestions and share them with the class. As with other areas of students' learning, giving students say on grading criteria enhances their control over their learning, which leads to increased engagement. Students' involvement results in a co-ownership of the criteria, and ensures that the criteria are clear and meaningful to the students. In addition, when students provide input in group settings, they get insight into the accuracy of their ideas and into what elements should be present in a high-quality persuasive essay. They also discover how close they are to meeting the teacher's standards. Listening to the comments and suggestions of their peers and teachers allows them to reevaluate their own ideas, as they determine what makes an excellent, average, or poor persuasive essay.

Following the suggestions included in Stage One, I brainstormed with my students about the elements of an effective persuasive essay to convince their classmates to buy a new car. They identified the following:

- facts;
- data;
- proof;
- statistics;
- study results;
- research findings;
- experts' opinions;
- evidence that I needed it;
- evidence that it would be good for me; and
- reasons why it would be fun to own one.

I then asked my students what criteria should be used to determine whether a persuasive essay is well written. They gave the following answers:

- good spelling and grammar;
- complete sentences and good punctuation;
- well-organized, logical argument;
- complete paragraphs; and
- a clear message about what they were trying to persuade us to do.

From my students' input, I put together a list of criteria (see figure 12.1) they can use to self-evaluate their essays.

Stage Two

Stage Two teaches students how to *apply the criteria* to their own work. Even though they co-own the categories, our students will need our help to apply the criteria effectively. I provide this help by fitting each category into a rubric format, using rubistar.com, which all of my students can use in their self-evaluations (see table 12.1).

After reviewing the rubric, I engage my students in a discussion of the rubric categories to make certain they understand each category and know how to apply the criteria to their papers. I then have the students use the

FIGURE 12.1
Criteria for evaluating a persuasive essay.

- Evidence or examples that support or reinforce the essay's persuasive message
- Accuracy of the data and facts used to persuade the audience
- Reliable sources identified as supporting the essay's message
- Complete sentences with accurate use of grammar and spelling
- Attention-grabbing opening paragraph that gets the audience interested in the message
- A clear expression of the message you are trying to persuade the audience to accept
- A thesis statement that introduces the topic and outlines the message
- An appropriate tone, style, and message for the audience you are addressing
- Clear and organized paragraph transitions that allow the reader to follow your message easily
- A final paragraph that summarizes the message and tries to close the deal

TABLE 12.1
Self-evaluation criteria

CATEGORY	4 *Above Standards*	3 *Meets Standards*	2 *Approaching Standards*	1 *Below Standards*
Attention Grabber	The introductory paragraph has a strong hook or attention grabber that is appropriate for the audience. This could be a strong statement or a relevant quotation, statistic, or question addressed to the reader.	The introductory paragraph has a hook or attention-grabber, but it is weak, rambling, or inappropriate for the audience.	The author has an interesting introductory paragraph, but the connection to the topic is not clear.	The introductory paragraph is not interesting, nor is it relevant to the topic.
Clear Message	The message statement provides a clear, strong statement of what you are trying to persuade us to do or believe.	The message statement provides a clear statement of what you are trying to persuade us to do or believe.	A message statement is present, but it is not clear what you are trying to persuade us to do or believe.	There is no message statement.
Focus or Thesis Statement	The thesis statement names the topic of the essay and outlines the main points to be discussed.	The thesis statement names the topic of the essay.	The thesis statement outlines some or all of the main points to be discussed but does not name the topic.	The thesis statement does not name the topic, nor does it preview what will be discussed.
Support for Position	Includes 4 or more pieces of evidence (facts, statistics, examples, real-life experiences) that support the position statement. The writer anticipates the reader's concerns, biases, or arguments and has provided at least 1 counterargument.	Includes 3 or more pieces of evidence (facts, statistics, examples, real-life experiences) that support the position statement.	Includes 2 pieces of evidence (facts, statistics, examples, real-life experiences) that support the position statement.	Includes 1 or no pieces of evidence (facts, statistics, examples, real-life experiences).
Evidence & Examples	All of the evidence and examples are specific and relevant, and explanations are given that show how each piece of evidence supports the position.	Most of the evidence and examples are specific and relevant, and explanations are given that show how each piece of evidence supports your position.	At least one of the pieces of evidence and examples is relevant and has an explanation that shows how that piece of evidence supports your position.	Evidence and examples are *not* relevant and/or are not explained.
Accuracy	All supportive facts and statistics are reported accurately.	Almost all supportive facts and statistics are reported accurately.	Most supportive facts and statistics are reported accurately.	Most supportive facts and statistics were reported inaccurately.
Transitions	A variety of thoughtful transitions between paragraphs are used. They clearly show how ideas are connected.	Transitions show how ideas are connected, but there is little variety.	Some transitions work well, but some connections between ideas are fuzzy.	The transitions between ideas are unclear or nonexistent.

(continued)

TABLE 12.1
(Continued)

CATEGORY	4 *Above Standards*	3 *Meets Standards*	2 *Approaching Standards*	1 *Below Standards*
Closing Paragraph	The conclusion is strong and leaves the reader solidly understanding the position. Effective restatement of the position statement begins the closing paragraph.	The conclusion is recognizable. Your position is restated within the first two sentences of the closing paragraph.	Your position is restated within the closing paragraph, but not near the beginning.	There is no conclusion—the paper just ends.
Sources	All sources used for quotes, statistics, and facts are credible and are cited correctly.	All sources used for quotes, statistics, and facts are credible, and most are cited correctly.	Most sources used for quotes, statistics, and facts are credible and cited correctly.	Many sources are suspect (not credible) *and/or* are not cited correctly.
Audience	Demonstrates a clear understanding of the potential reader and uses appropriate vocabulary and arguments. Anticipates questions and provides thorough answers.	Demonstrates a general understanding of the potential reader and uses vocabulary and arguments appropriate for that audience.	Demonstrates some understanding of the potential reader and uses arguments appropriate for that audience.	It is not clear whom the author is writing for.
Sentence Structure	All sentences are well constructed with varied structure.	Most sentences are well constructed, and there is some varied sentence structure in the essay.	Most sentences are well constructed, but there is no variation in structure.	Most sentences are not well constructed or varied.
Grammar & Spelling	You make no errors in grammar or spelling that distract the reader from the content.	You make 1–2 errors in grammar or spelling that distract the reader from the content.	You make 3–4 errors in grammar or spelling that distract the reader from the content.	You make more than 4 errors in grammar or spelling that distract the reader from the content.
Capitalization & Punctuation	You make no errors in capitalization or punctuation, so the essay is exceptionally easy to read.	You make 1–2 errors in capitalization or punctuation, but the essay is still easy to read.	You make a few errors in capitalization and/or punctuation that catch the reader's attention and interrupt the flow.	You make several errors in capitalization and/or punctuation that catch the reader's attention and interrupt the flow.

rubric to evaluate their persuasive essays, scoring themselves on each category and bringing their results back to class.

Stage Three

In Stage Three, students receive feedback on the effectiveness of their self-evaluations. Students' initial comprehension of the criteria and its application are likely to be imperfect (Rolheiser & Ross, 2000). One of the best ways to help our students determine the accuracy of their self-assessment is to share peer evaluations of the essay as well as our evaluation, all using the same rubric. Providing data for comparison helps students develop accurate self-evaluations.

Stage Four

The final stage teaches students how to develop productive goals and action plans for improvement. The most difficult part of teaching students how to evaluate their work is providing support and advice as they use self-evaluative data to set new goals and levels of effort (Rolheiser & Ross, 2000, p. 4).One approach is to have students examine the strategies, skills, effort, and time they put into the essay in the context of their own findings and the feedback from their peers and teacher. This process will either confirm that their strategy and effort were on target (if the work was evaluated positively), or indicate that they need to rethink their strategy and effort (if the evaluations suggest that the work fell short of their goal). Self-evaluation allows our students to develop a sense of the skills, strategies, effort, and time needed for each new project they face. By using self-evaluation regularly, even if it does not involve detailed criteria, students will develop both a mechanism to improve the quality of all their work and a lifelong learning skill and career enhancement tool that will be vital to their long-term success.

Evaluating Others Effectively

When my son started Little League Baseball, it was not uncommon to see many of the young boys and girls strike out. Most often when a child did strike out, the parents and coaches in attendance would yell, "good try," "good effort," or "you'll get 'em next time." These words of encouragement seemed to be a very appropriate response. However, some children struck out every time without ever taking the bat off their shoulder. These children, in fact, did not give it a good try or a good effort. I often felt that the "good try" message being sent to these players somehow cheated and misled them. The feedback they were getting would not lead to any improvement, especially since it was inaccurate. Additionally, the message to the other players on the team was that making someone feel good is more important than giving useful feedback that could lead to improvement. I am not some kind of sports parent obsessed with winning. I am, however, interested in helping young people improve their lives by accepting feedback and suggestions that address their weaknesses and suggest, in a positive way, how they might do better. This is the same attitude I expect of my students when they are reviewing one another's work as a means to improve. Little will be gained if every piece of work or in-class presentation receives a "good job" from the entire class, regardless of its quality.

Giving Meaningful Feedback

I spent a year chairing a committee whose purpose was to make suggestions about improving the Student Assessment of Instruction Questionnaire Ferris State students use to give feedback to professors on their teaching. The committee was unsuccessful in meeting its charge; we were unable to agree on what parts of the teaching process students were informed enough about to offer meaningful feedback on. We also could not agree on common definitions for the key words used in the questions. For example, what did we mean by supportive, organized, available, caring, helpful, and challenging? In spite of our lack of progress, my work on this committee was not a complete waste of time because it helped me clarify what my own students would need to know if they were to become effective evaluators of each other's work. I knew I would need to ensure that they had the skills and knowledge to give meaningful feedback, and that they understood and were comfortable with the agreed-upon meanings of the words being used in the evaluations.

A Rationale for Peer Evaluation

Peer evaluation is a win-win situation for both the reviewer and the feedback recipient. Those receiving the feedback get to consider their self-assessment in a new light. By having others assess their work, point out issues, and offer suggestions, students will learn how to improve the overall quality of their work. The reviewer benefits by developing the ability to recognize good work from bad, frame feedback in clear and helpful ways, and deliver feedback in a positive manner. All of these skills will benefit learners for the rest of their lives.

There are four basic steps to facilitate the effective use of peer evaluation. The first is to clearly define what areas of the work under review are to be evaluated. These areas must be congruent with the skills and knowledge of the students doing the review. For example, if students are asked to read one another's persuasive essays, the following questions would be appropriate:

1. Was the subject/topic of the essay clear?
2. Were arguments or evidence used to persuade you?
3. Could you tell if the arguments or evidence were true?
4. Were you able to follow the logic of the arguments/evidence throughout the whole paper?
5. Were you persuaded?
6. If you lost track of how the arguments or evidence were supporting the topic, where in the paper did this occur?
7. Did you notice any spelling errors?

Examples of inappropriate questions might include:

1. Was there a focus or thesis statement?
2. Were there thoughtful transitions between the ideas introduced?
3. Was the sequencing of the arguments or evidence logical?
4. Were there grammatical errors/punctuation errors?

You may want to include your students in the discussion about appropriate questions. They can provide good ideas and will be able to define areas in which they are capable of giving helpful feedback.

The second step in using peer evaluation successfully is to define the language that will be used to give the feedback. This includes both the language used in the questions/rubric and the evaluative language, including such words as excellent, good, average, poor, or incomplete. Standardizing language will lead to feedback that is clear and helpful to all of the students.

A third step in this process is to establish classroom etiquette for giving feedback. This means that all class members agree to give feedback that can be used to improve the work of others, and to do so in a positive manner focusing on the work, not the person. An example of inappropriate personalized feedback would be, "You must not have worked very hard on this paper because I can't understand any of your arguments." A more appropriate response might be, "I am unable to follow your argument from paragraph to paragraph. Can you explain it to me?"

Fourth, and last, the feedback must focus on a few important aspects of the work. We must remember that our students are novices at giving feedback. Using a rubric or set of questions that provides focus to the peer review process will improve feedback tremendously. If an entire class is giving feedback, different members of the class can focus on different aspects of the work to make certain all important areas have been reviewed. This approach helps focus students by making each of them responsible for a particular aspect of the work under review.

Giving Teachers Meaningful Feedback

For learner-centered teaching to be effective, we must involve our students actively and regularly in the classroom feedback and assessment processes as well as in our day-to-day teaching practices. By asking students to be partners in assessing the effectiveness of our learner-centered practice, we create a model of continuous improvement that will lead to optimal learning. Seventy years of research strongly suggest that students' assessments of teaching practice, when done well, can yield meaningful and constructive feedback (Ory & Ryan, 2001). Some of the most effective ways to gather students' feedback are discussed in the next few pages.

Small-Group Instructional Diagnosis

A small-group instructional diagnosis (SGID), a formative assessment of learning practice that usually takes place between the 4th and 6th weeks of the semester, is conducted by someone other than the instructor (usually someone from the faculty development center). It involves asking students 3 questions about how they see their learning progressing thus far in the semester. The unique component of an SGID is that the students answer the questions in groups, and the only answers reported are those that are reached by consensus. This practice eliminates individual complaining and focuses the feedback on those areas of the course that students can agree are effective or need improvement. The three questions used (these may vary from institution to institution) are:

1. What do you like about the course and course instruction?
2. What would you change about the course or course instruction?
3. What would you do to make the course better for you and the instructor?

Some institutions use the question, What would you delete from the course? as the third question. The student groups agree on the answers to each question, and the facilitator asks each group to report one answer for each question, until all answers have been recorded. The answers are displayed for students to see.

In the next step, the students vote on whether they agree with each answer. The feedback the professor receives is given as a percentage of students who agreed with each answer. This feedback gives a much clearer picture of what the students think of the course and the instruction than do individual student comments. The professor received this confidential feedback, and a consultation is available, but not required, to discuss the findings.

Most faculty development centers have individuals available to conduct an SGID. It usually takes 20–40 minutes, depending on the number of students in the class. The SGID takes place early in the semester so meaningful changes to the course, if warranted, can occur. In addition to the quality feedback faculty receive, students are often impressed that their teacher is willing to listen to their views and to make meaningful changes to improve their learning. As a result, this opportunity for students to express their opinions also increases their control over their learning. This sense of control often leads to greater trust of the professor and a greater willingness to engage in the learning process.

Classroom Assessment Techniques

In 1993, Thomas Angelo and K. Patricia Cross wrote a handbook, titled *Classroom Assessment Techniques* (CATs), to help teachers gather feedback on whether and how their students are learning. The book also helps teachers assess the effectiveness of their teaching methods. CATs are easy and effective ways to discover the gaps that often exist between what was taught and what was learned. As a parent, I regularly discovered gaps between what I thought I said to my daughter, and what she actually heard. I would say, "Honey, clean up your room," and she would hear, "Go watch television." CATs ensure that what we think we said was really what students heard (p. 3).

A simple example is a CAT, called the Muddiest Point (Angelo & Cross, 1993, p. 154). Students are asked to briefly jot down what is still not clear to them from the day's learning activity. The teacher uses the feedback to determine whether the information needs to be clarified. The feedback lets the teacher know instantly whether students understood the important ideas and concepts introduced that day. By asking our students to report, we can make the adjustments needed to optimize their learning.

A variety of CATs can be found in Angelo and Cross's book, but you can also develop your own based on the specific information you are seeking from your students. In either case, the value of the information increases greatly if we help our students learn to express their feedback in precise and meaningful ways. For example, if we ask our students whether the images used in a lecture were helpful in their understanding and they say they were not, this feedback is of limited use because we still don't know why the images weren't helpful. If we teach our students to be precise, we can get feedback such as, "There was too much information on the concept map you used for me to see the relationships you were talking about." Now, that's the kind of feedback we can put to practical use to improve future teaching and learning. When asking students to provide feedback about their learning experience, we should model the kinds of responses that are most useful to us. It is of little value for them to tell us that our teaching "sucks," or that it's "awesome." These comments are ambiguous and offer no substantive information on which to build.

Seeking Students' Feedback

The following examples represent some useful methods for soliciting student feedback.

Homework Feedback

When giving a homework assignment, ask students to tell you if the assignment was useful in helping them understand and learn the material. This simple question will help to reduce the number of assignments viewed as busywork and to improve the accuracy of matching students' assignments with the leaning outcome of the course. It will also help develop a file drawer full of assignments that we know to be effective for learning. Students' metacognitive skills will be improved by this activity, too, since we ask them to evaluate whether the assigned activities helped them learn. The result is greater student awareness of what types of learning activities work best for them.

Talking With Students Before and After Class

Letting our students know that we want their input and feedback is only meaningful if we are available to receive it. One of the signs that we are genuinely interested in what our students have to say is being available before and after class for informal conversations. Not only will we learn a great deal about our students' learning concerns, but we will also build connections with them that will increase the level of trust between us, leading to a better learning environment. Our availability sends a powerful message that we care, are interested in their learning success, and want them to be partners in the learning process. This will build a true community of learners.

Replying to E-mail

Another way to encourage students' involvement in their own learning is by asking for course feedback via e-mail. If encouraged to do so, many students, who otherwise might be hesitant to do so, are willing to express their concerns and questions to us electronically. Some students may need more encouragement than others since they are unaccustomed to giving feedback to teachers. Students need constant reminding that we want to hear their ideas. It is also a good idea to announce to students the time frame for responding to their e-mails so they don't interpret a few days' silence as a slight.

Office Hours

One of the first examples I use to help faculty understand what is meant by learner-centered teaching is setting office hours. As I mentioned earlier, teachers who set their office hours after polling their students about optimal times are engaging in a learner-centered action. By being available when we say we will, we send a message that we care and are trustworthy. One-on-one meetings are among the best ways to get feedback on the effectiveness of the learning process.

Giving Feedback Is a Lifelong Process

With our help, our students can learn to be effective evaluators of their own learning, the work of their peers, and our teaching. Knowing how to give fair, clear, and meaningful feedback in a way that allows others to improve and make changes is a skill that will serve our students well for the rest of their lives.

Research Report Writing and Reading Assignments Report Writing

Parts of a Research Report

Cover Sheet

This should contain some or all of the following: full title of the report; your name; the name of the unit of which the project is a part; the name of the institution; the date.

Title Page

Full title of the report; your name; acknowledgments; a thank you to the people who helped you.

Contents or Table of Contents

Contents includes the headings and subheadings used in the report with their page numbers.

Introduction

This is the overview of the whole report. It should let the reader see, in advance, what is in the report. This includes what you set out to do, how reviewing the literature focused or narrowed your research, the relation of the methodology you chose to your aims, a summary of your findings, and an analysis of your findings.

Aims and Purpose of the Report

Why did you do the work? What problem were you investigating? If you are not including a literature review, mention here the other research relevant to your work.

Literature Review

This should help you put your research into the context of other research and explain its importance. Include only the books and articles that relate directly to your topic.

Methodology

Methodology deals with the methods and principles used in the research. In the methodology chapter you explain the method/s you used for the research and why you thought they were appropriate. Examples include surveys, test results, and interviews.

Results or Findings

What did you find out? Give a clear presentation of your results. Show the essential data and calculations here; you may want to use tables, graphs, and figures.

Analysis and Discussion

Interpret your results. What do you make of them? How do they compare with those of others who have done research in this area?

Conclusions

What do you conclude? You should briefly summarize the main conclusions that you discussed under "Results." Were you able to answer some or all of the questions you raised in your aims?

Recommendations

Make your recommendations. These can be positive or negative suggestions for either action or further research.

Appendix

You may not need an appendix, or you may need several.

Bibliography

List all the sources to which you refer in the body of the report. You may also list all the relevant sources you consulted even if you did not quote them.

Writing a Review of an Assigned Reading

There is no one correct way to develop a piece of writing. Below is an example of one possible way to organize a paper once the information has been gathered from the readings.

1. When you have gathered all your notes (cards), sort them into piles of what you think might be the main topics or subtopics you will cover.

2. If one note card has several ideas, photocopy it or cut the different ideas apart. Be sure to note the original reference on each part.

3. Take each pile and sort it in an order that makes sense.

4. You will want to add more slips with your own ideas if these were to be included.

5. Now you are ready to write your review.

6. Start by introducing the topic and giving a brief statement of the few main topics that you will cover in the review.

7. Take your topic piles one by one and write an explanation of the ideas you want to present. Use headings (which may correspond to your piles) and guide the reader through the material.

8. If possible, stop at times, perhaps at the end of each topic, to mention the main relevant ideas and how they fit together.

9. Once you have gone through all of your piles, write at least a brief conclusion summarizing the main findings and conclusions.

As with all writing, leave it, then reread, edit, and revise what you have written, to make sure that it makes sense and flows in a way that will allow the reader to understand what you are tying to convey.

Problem-Solving Process

Define the Problem

The problem can already exist, or the students may need to define it. In the latter case, the following questions are helpful:

1. What makes you think there is a problem?
2. What or who is being affected by the problem?
3. What is or is not happening that may be causing the problem?
4. Do others see the same problem you do?
5. Try to write a description of the problem.

Explore Causes for the Problem

1. What do you think are the causes?
2. What do your peers or colleagues think are the causes?
3. What do experts say about the possible causes?
4. What do the data point to as causes?

Identify Resources Needed to Help Develop Possible Solutions

1. Whom do you need to know more about?
2. What do you need to know more about?
3. Where might you find the who or what?

Suggest Possible Solutions

1. Brainstorm likely solutions from the information gathered.
2. Identify best possible solution from all generated.
3. List pluses and minuses of each possible solution.
4. Identify possible side effects or concerns of each solution.

Select a Solution

1. Select the solution most likely to fix the problem with the fewest minuses or side effects.
2. Make certain you have identified the resources needed to implement the solution, including time.

Plan the Implementation of the Solution

1. What will the situation look like if this solution is implemented?
2. What is the order of the steps to implementation?
3. Who will carry out the solution?

Evaluate the Effectiveness of the Solution

1. Is the solution working?
2. Does the solution need adjusting?
3. Is the solution following the recommended steps?
4. Are the resources needed for the solution to work available?
5. Is the problem solved?

Feedback Rubric

Rubric for Giving Students Feedback on Their Teaching

CATEGORY	4	3	2	1
Vocabulary	Defined all new vocabulary accurately.	Defined most of the new vocabulary accurately.	Only defined a few of the new vocabulary accurately.	Failed to define the new vocabulary.
Preparedness	Student seems completely prepared.	Student seems pretty prepared.	Student is somewhat prepared.	Student does not seem at all prepared to teach.
Content	Shows a full understanding of the topic.	Shows a good understanding of the topic.	Shows a good understanding of parts of the topic.	Does not seem to understand the topic very well.
Stays on Topic	Stays on topic all (100%) of the time.	Stays on topic most (99–90%) of the time.	Stays on topic some (89–75%) of the time.	It was hard to tell what the topic was.
Comprehension	Student is able to accurately answer almost all questions about the topic posed by classmates.	Student is able to accurately answer most questions about the topic posed by classmates.	Student is able to accurately answer a few questions about the topic posed by classmates.	Student is unable to accurately answer questions about the topic posed by classmates.
Enthusiasm	Made good attempt to generate a strong interest and enthusiasm about the topic in others.	Made some attempt to generate interest and enthusiasm about the topic in others.	Generated only a little enthusiasm for learning the topic.	Did not generate much interest in topic being presented.
Use of Images	Nice balance of text and images in aiding understanding of the material.	Nice overall use of images, but too few were used.	A few images were used to help in understanding.	No images were used in the teaching.
Beginning and Ending	Clearly had an introduction to the topic and a summary or review of the topic at the end.	Had only a brief introduction and brief conclusion to the teaching.	Had only an introduction but no ending activities (or vice versa).	Had no beginning or ending to the teaching.
Class Involved in Learning	Got the whole class actively involved in learning the material.	Got most of the class actively involved in learning the material.	Got only a few members of the class involved in learning the material.	Had no class involvement.
Handout	Handout was well organized and aided students' learning.	Handout was generally helpful to students' learning.	Handout was of little value in aiding students' learning.	No handout was given.

APPENDIX D

Sample Rubrics

Collaboration Rubric

Name _____

	Beginning 1	Developing 2	Accomplished 3	Exemplary 4	Score
Contribute					
Research & Gather Information	Does not collect any information that relates to the topic.	Collects very little information—some relates to the topic.	Collects some basic information—most relates to the topic.	Collects a great deal of information—all relates to the topic.	
Share Information	Does not relay any information to teammates.	Relays very little information—some relates to the topic.	Relays some basic information—most relates to the topic.	Relays a great deal of information—all relates to the topic.	
Be Punctual	Does not hand in any assignments.	Hands in most assignments late.	Hands in most assignments on time.	Hands in all assignments on time.	
Take Responsibility					
Fulfill Team Role's Duties	Does not perform any duties of assigned team role.	Performs very few duties.	Performs nearly all duties.	Performs all duties of assigned team role.	
Share Equally	Always relies on others to do the work.	Rarely does the assigned work—often needs reminding.	Usually does the assigned work—rarely needs reminding.	Always does the assigned work without having to be reminded.	
Value Others' Viewpoints					
Listen to Other Teammates	Is always talking—never allows anyone else to speak.	Usually doing most of the talking—rarely allows others to speak.	Listens, but sometimes talks too much.	Listens and speaks a fair amount.	
Cooperate With Teammates	Usually argues with teammates.	Sometimes argues with teammates.	Rarely argues with teammates.	Never argues with teammates.	
Make Fair Decisions	Usually wants to have things his or her way.	Often sides with friends instead of considering all views.	Usually considers all views.	Always helps team to reach a fair decision.	
				Total	

Presentation Rubric

Evaluating Student Presentations

Developed by Information Technology Evaluation Services, North Carolina Department of Public Instruction

	1	2	3	4	*Total*
Organization	Audience cannot understand presentation because there is no sequence of information.	Audience has difficulty following presentation because student jumps around.	Student presents information in logical sequence that audience can follow.	Student presents information in logical, interesting sequence that audience can follow.	
Subject knowledge	Student does not have grasp of information; student cannot answer questions about subject.	Student is uncomfortable with information and is able to answer only rudimentary questions.	Student is at ease with expected answers to all questions, but fails to elaborate.	Student demonstrates full knowledge (more than required) by answering all class questions with explanations and elaboration.	
Graphics	Student uses superfluous graphics or none at all.	Student occasionally uses graphics that rarely support text and presentation.	Student's graphics relate to text and presentation.	Student's graphics explain and reinforce screen text and presentation.	
Mechanics	Student's presentation has four or more spelling and/or grammatical errors.	Presentation has three misspellings and/or grammatical errors.	Presentation has no more than two misspellings and/or grammatical errors.	Presentation has no misspellings or grammatical errors.	
Eye Contact	Student reads all of report with no eye contact.	Student occasionally uses eye contact, but still reads most of report.	Student maintains eye contact most of the time, but frequently returns to notes.	Student maintains eye contact with audience, seldom returning to notes.	
Elocution	Student mumbles, pronounces terms incorrectly, and speaks too quietly for students in the back of class to hear.	Student's voice is low. Student pronounces terms incorrectly. Audience members have difficulty hearing presentation.	Student's voice is clear. Student pronounces most words correctly. Most audience members can hear presentation.	Student uses a clear voice and correct, precise pronunciation of terms so that all audience members can hear presentation.	

Total Points:

Group Project Rubric

CATEGORY	4	3	2	1
Contributions	Routinely provides useful ideas when participating in the group and in classroom discussion. A definite leader who contributes a lot of effort.	Usually provides useful ideas when participating in the group and in classroom discussion. A strong group member who tries hard.	Sometimes provides useful ideas when participating in the group and in classroom discussion. A satisfactory group member who does what is required.	Rarely provides useful ideas when participating in the group and in classroom discussion. May refuse to participate.
Time Management	Routinely uses time well throughout the project to ensure things get done on time. Group does not have to adjust deadlines or work responsibilities because of this person's procrastination.	Usually uses time well throughout the project, but may have procrastinated on one thing. Group does not have to adjust deadlines or work responsibilities because of this person's procrastination.	Tends to procrastinate, but always gets things done by the deadlines. Group does not have to adjust deadlines or work responsibilities because of this person's procrastination.	Rarely gets things done by the deadlines *and* group has to adjust deadlines or work responsibilities because of this person's inadequate time management.
Quality of Work	Provides work of the highest quality.	Provides high-quality work.	Provides work that occasionally needs to be checked/redone by other group members to ensure quality.	Provides work that usually needs to be checked/redone by others to ensure quality.
Attitude	Is never publicly critical of the project or the work of others. Always has a positive attitude about the task(s).	Is rarely publicly critical of the project or the work of others. Often has a positive attitude about the task(s).	Is occasionally publicly critical of the project or the work of other members of the group. Usually has a positive attitude about the task(s).	Is often publicly critical of the project or the work of other members of the group. Often has a negative attitude about the task(s).

Student Background Questionnaire

Demographics

1. What barriers exist in your current living situation that could prevent you from succeeding in this course?

   Work/job
   Children/daycare
   Transportation
   Finances
   Health issues
   None
   Other

2. What plan do you have for removing the barriers listed above?
3. What is your current age?

   17–22
   23–30
   31 and older

4. What are your ideal meeting times if you are given group work outside of class?

   Evenings
   Afternoons
   Mornings
   Anytime (check all that apply)

5. What are your best days for meeting outside of class? Check all that apply.

   Sunday
   Monday
   Tuesday
   Wednesday
   Thursday

Friday
Saturday

6. Are you currently employed?

   Yes
   No

   If yes how many hours per week?

   1–10
   11–15
   16–20
   21–30
   Full time

7. Are you the first person in your family to attend college?

   Yes
   No

8. How many credit hours are you taking this semester?

   1–8
   9–12
   13–16
   17–20

9. What is your current career interest?

   Health field
   Technology field
   Business field
   Education
   Professional (Pharmacy or Optometry)
   Other

General Skills

1. What was the last course you took in this field of study?
2. When did you take it?

   Last semester
   One year ago

Three semesters ago
Two years ago or longer

3. What grade did you earn in that course?

    A
    B
    C
    D
    F

4. Did you take courses related to this course in high school?

    Yes
    No

5. Do you have work experience or internship experience related to this course?

    Yes
    No

6. Do you have a family member or relative with work experience related to this course?

    Yes
    No

7. To what extent do you enjoy learning about the subject of this course?

    Enjoy it a great deal
    Somewhat enjoy it
    Don't enjoy it

8. How confident are you that you will do well in this course?

    Very confident
    Somewhat confident
    Not confident

9. What grade do you intend on earning in this course?

    A
    B

C
D
F

Views of Learning

1. What are your strengths as a learner?
2. What are your weaknesses as a learner?
3. What are your reasons for taking this course?

   Required in my major
   Elective I need
   Interested in the subject
   Need it to get in my program
   Other

4. How useful do you think this course is in helping you reach your career/learning goals?

   Very useful
   Useful
   Not useful
   Uncertain

5. How do you feel about learning in groups?

   Like it
   It's OK
   Don't like it

6. How would you describe your learning preference?

   Like to learn alone
   Like to learn with others
   Both are fine

7. How confident are you speaking in front of others?

   Very confident
   Confident
   Somewhat confident
   Not confident

8. How many hours on average do you study per week?

    0–5
    6–10
    11–15
    16–20
    21 or more

9. Do you own a computer or have easy access to one?

    Yes
    No

10. Do you have easy access to a high-speed Internet connection?

    Yes
    No

11. How proficient are you in your computer skills?

    Microsoft Word
      Very good
      Average
      Not so good
      Have never used it

    PowerPoint
      Very good
      Average
      Not so good
      Have never used it

    Microsoft Excel
      Very good
      Average
      Not so good
      Have never used it

12. How often do you use the Internet to help you with school work?

    Often
    Sometimes
    Rarely

13. If you need help passing a course, how likely are you to seek tutoring?

> Very likely
> Likely
> Not likely

Websites on Learning How to Give Effective Criticism

- Giving constructive criticism with aplomb. (includes guidelines for preparing creative criticism) (Handling Criticism, part 1)
  From: Medical Laboratory Observer | Date: 3/1/1991 | Author: Harmon, Shirley
  http://www.encyclopedia.com/doc/1G1-10529979.html
- Grand Valley State University's Nonprofit Good Practice Guide
  http://www.npgoodpractice.org/Search/Default.aspx?type = topic&
  topicareaid = 638
- The 4-1-1 On Constructive Criticism By: Jamie Walters Published August 2001
  http://www.inc.com/articles/2001/08/23257.html
- Effective Interpersonal/Intrateam Communication
  http://www.foundationcoalition.org

REFERENCES

ACT, Inc. (2006). ACT, American College Testing Program, *Reading between the lines: What ACT reveals about college readiness in reading.* Iowa City, IA: Author.

ACT News. (1998, April 1). New low for college graduation rate, but dropout picture brighter. Retrieved February 7, 2007, from http://www.act.org/news/releases/1998/04–01–98.html

Airasian, P. W. (1991). *Classroom assessment.* New York: McGraw-Hill.

American Institute of Physics (1998), *Misconceptions about physics,* retrieved December 11, 2006 from http://www.aip.org

Ambedkar, B. R. (1955). Thoughts on linguistic states. Retrieved March 7, 2008, from http://www.ambedkar.org/ambcd/05A.%20Thoughts%20on%20Linguistic%20States %20Par t%20I.htm#p01

Ames, C. (1992). Classrooms: Goals, structures, and student motivation. *Journal of Educational Psychology, 84,* 261–271.

Angelo, T., & Cross, K. P. (1993). *Classroom assessment techniques: A handbook for college teachers* (2nd ed.). San Francisco: Jossey-Bass.

Appleby, D. (2001). The covert curriculum: The lifelong learning skills you can learn in college. *Eye on Psi Chi: The National Honors Society in Psychology, 5*(3), 28–31.

Arendal, L., & Mann, V. (2000). *Fast ForWord reading: Why it works.* Berkeley, CA: Scientific Learning Corporation.

Armstrong, T. (1994). Multiple intelligences: Seven ways to approach curriculum. *Educational Leadership, 52*(3), 26.

Arter, D. R. (1994). In 192ISO 9000 in construction. *Journal of Construction Education, 2*(3), pp. 182–192.

Associated Press. (2001, August 16). College graduation rate below fifty percent. Retrieved September 9, 2007, from http://www.cnn.com/2001/fyi/teachers.ednews/08/15/college.dropout.ap/index

Astin, A. (1998). The changing American college student: Thirty-year trends, 1966–1996. *The Review of Higher Education, 21*(2), 115–135.

Ausubel, D. P. (1960). The use of advanced organizers in the learning and retention of meaningful verbal material. *Journal of Educational Psychology, 51,* 267–272.

Baker, F. (2003). *Service learning.* Keynote speech for Lilly West Conference, Pomona, CA.

Bangert-Drowns, R. L., Kulick, J. A., & Morgan, M. T. (1991). The instructional effect of feedback in test-like events. *Review of Educational Research, 16*(2), 213–238.

Barr, B., & Tagg, J. (1995). From teaching to learning: A new paradigm for under-graduate education [Abstract]. *Change* (November/December), 13–25.

Baxter-Magolda, M. (1992). *Knowing and reasoning in college: Gender-related patterns in students' intellectual development.* San Francisco: Jossey-Bass.

Berry, B. (2005). Recruiting and retaining board-certified teachers for hard-to-staff schools. *Phi Delta Kappan, 85*(4), 290–297.

Bickmore-Brand, J. (1996). Bickmore-brand's literacy and learning principles. Step-ping out: Literacy and learning strategies. In S. Downes. (2000). Giving control to students: But will they pick up the ball and run? In A. Herrmann & M. M. Kulski (Eds.), *Flexible futures in tertiary teaching.* Proceedings of the 9th Annual Teaching Learning Forum, February 2–4, 2000. Perth: Curtin University of Technology.

Biemiller, A., & Meichenbaum, D. (1992). The nature and nurture of the self-directed learner. *Educational Leadership, 50*(2), 75–80.

Bigelow, J. D. (1996). Management skill teachers speak out. *Journal of Management Education, 20,* 298–318.

Binet, A. (1911). *Modern ideas about children (Les idées moderne sur les enfants).* Paris: Flammarion.

Bjork, D. R. (1994). Memory and metamemory: Considerations in the training of human beings. In J. Metcalfe & A. P. Shimamura (Eds.), *Metacognition: Knowing about knowing* (pp. 185–205). Cambridge, MA: MIT Press.

Black, P., & Wiliam, D. (1998). Inside the black box: Raising standards through classroom assessment. *Phi Delta Kappan, 80*(2), 139–144, 146–148.

Boud, D. J., Keogh, R., & Walker, D. (1985). What is reflection in learning? In D. J. Boud, R. Keogh, & D. Walker (Eds.), *Reflection: Turning experience into learning* (pp. 7–17). London: Kogan Page.

Bransford, J., Brown, A. L., & Cocking, R. R. (Eds.). (2000). *How people learn: Brain, mind, experience, and school* (Expanded ed.). Washington, DC: National Academy Press.

Bransford, J. D., Franks, J. J., Vye, N. J., & Sherwood, R. D. (1989). New ap-proaches to instruction: Because wisdom can't be told. In S. Vosniadou & A. Ortony (Eds.), *Similarity and analogical reasoning* (pp. 470–497). New York: Cambridge University Press.

Bransford, J., Sherwood, R., & Hasselbring, T. (1988). The video revolution and its effects on development: Some initial thoughts. In G. Foreman & P. Pufall (Eds.),

Constructivism in the computer age (pp. 173–201). Hillsdale, NJ: Lawrence Erlbaum Associates.

Brown, J. S., Collins, A., & Duguid, P. (1989). Situated cognition and the culture of learning. *Educational Researcher, 18*, 32–42.

Bryan, William Jennings. Retrieved March 3, 2007, from http://www.brainyquote.com/quotes/authors/w/william_jennings_bryan.html

Bryson, B. (1999). *A walk in the woods.* New York: Random House.

Buechler, Mark. (2000). *Closing the achievement gap at the secondary level through comprehensive school reform. A working conference. Conference proceedings.* Atlanta, GA., December 1–2, 2000.

Burnaford, G., Aprill, A., & Weiss, C. (2001). *Renaissance in the classroom: Arts integration and meaningful learning.* Mahwah, NJ: Erlbaum.

Caine, G., & Caine, R. (1994). *Making connections: Teaching and the human brain.* New York: Addison Wesley.

Caine, R., & Caine, G. (1997). *Education on the edge of possibility.* Alexandria, VA: Association for Supervision and Curriculum Development.

Carey, Kevin. (2005). Finish line: Higher college graduation rates are within our reach. A report for the Educational Trust. Retrieved March 3, 2007, from http://www2.edtrust.org/NR/rdonlyres/12656449–03FD-4F3F-A617–920E58F009C0/one ...step_from.pdf

Carnegie Council on Policy Studies in Higher Education. (1993). *Federal reorganization: Education and scholarship.* A report of the Carnegie Council on Policy Studies in Higher Education. Berkeley, CA: Author.

Casey, Mary. (2002). *Capitalizing on competition: The economic underpinnings of SPARC.* Washington, DC: Scholarly Publishing and Academic Resources Coalition. Retrieved March 3, 2006, from http://www.arl.org/sparc/publications/case_capitalizing_2002.html

Chicago Arts Partnerships in Education. (2001). Introduction. In G. E. Burnaford, A. Aprill, & C. Weiss (Eds.), *Renaissance in the classroom: Arts integration and meaningful learning* (p. xxxv). Mahwah, NJ: Erlbaum

Cobb, P. (1994). Where is the mind? Constructivist and socio-cultural perspectives on mathematical development. *Educational Researcher, 23*(7), 13–20.

Cohn, E., & Geske, T. G. (1992). *Private non-monetary returns to investment in higher education: The economics of American higher education.* Boston: Kluwer Academic.

Colvin, G. (2006). What it takes to be great. *Fortune, 154*(9), 88.

Covington, M. (2000). Goal theory, motivation and social achievement: An integrative review. *Annual Review of Psychology, 51*, 171–200.

Covington, M. V. (1992). *Making the grade: A self worth perspective on motivation and school reform.* New York: Cambridge University Press.

Cross, P. K. (2001). *Motivation, er . . . will that be on the test?* Oral presentation given to the League for Innovation in the Community College, Mission Viejo, CA.

Darling-Hammond, L. (1997). *The right to learn: A blueprint for creating schools that work.* San Francisco: Jossey-Bass.

DeBard, R. (2004). Millennials coming to college. *New Directions for Student Services, 106,* 33–45.

DeBra, P. M. (1996). Hypermedia structures and systems. Retrieved August 24, 2006, from http://wwwis.win.tue.nl/2L670/static

Deci, E. L., & Ryan, R. M. (1991). A motivational approach to self: Integration in personality. *Nebraska Symposium on Motivation, 38,* 237–288.

Dewey, J. (1997). *How we think.* New York: Dover Publications.

Doyle, T. (2008). Downloadable PowerPoint presentation. http://www.ferris.edu/htmls/academics/center/Teaching_and_Learning_Tips/T_LHome.htm Click on "Time Management (powerpoint)."

Doyle, T., & Marcinkiewicz, H. (2004). *New faculty development: Planning an ideal program.* Stillwater, OK: New Forums Press.

Dweck, C. (2000). *Self-theories: Their role in motivation, personality, and development.* Philadelphia: Psychology Press Publishing Office.

Dweck, C. (2006). *Mindset: The new psychology of success.* New York: Random House.

Elawar, M. C., & Corno, L. (1985). A factorial experiment in teachers' written feedback on student homework: Changing teacher behavior a little rather than a lot. *Journal of Educational Psychology, 77*(2), 162–173.

Ertmer, P. A., & Newby, T. J. (1996). The expert learner: strategic, self-regulated, and reflective. *Instructional Science, 24*(1), 1–24.

Evers, F. T., Rush, J., & Berdrow, I. (1998). *The bases of competence: Skills for lifelong learning and employability* (1st ed.). San Francisco: Jossey-Bass.

First Hand Learning Inc. (2007). First hand learning, 1998. Retrieved December 11, 2006, from http://firsthandlearning.org/

Fitts, J. D. (1998). *A comparison of locus of control and achievement among remedial summer bridge and non-bridge students in community colleges in New Jersey* (ERIC Document Reproduction Service No. 315102).

Gardiner, L. F. (1994). *Redesigning higher education: Producing dramatic gains in student learning.* Washington, DC: Graduate School of Education and Human Development, George Washington University.

Gardner, H. (1993). *Frames of mind: The theory of multiple intelligences* (2nd ed.). New York: Basic Books.

Gladwell, M. (2000). *The tipping point: How little things can make a big difference.* New York: Little, Brown and Company.

Glasser, William. (1990). *The quality school.* New York: Harper & Row.

Goldberg, E. (2002). *The executive brain: Frontal lobes and the civilized mind.* New York: Oxford University Press.

Goldman, Daniel. (1996). *Emotional intelligence.* New York: Bantam.

Goldman, D., Boyatzis, R., & McKee, A. (2002). *Primal leadership: Realizing the power of emotional intelligence.* Boston: Harvard Business Press.

Gotwals, J., et al. (1997). *Appendix D. Report of the Subcommittee on Teaching and Learning in the Digital Age.* Atlanta, GA: Emory University. Retrieved October 2, 2006, from http://www.emory.edu/TEACHING/Report/AppendixD.html

Graybiel, A. (2005). Activity of striatal neurons reflects dynamic encoding and re-coding of procedural memories. *Nature, 437,* 1158–1161.

Hagen, A. S., & Weinstein, C. E. (1995). Achievement goals, self-regulated learning, and the role of classroom context. In P. R. Pintrich (Ed.), *New directions for teaching and learning* (63rd ed., pp. 43–56). San Francisco: Jossey-Bass.

Hamann, S. B., Ely, T. D., Grafton, S. T., & Kilts, C. D. (1999). Amygdala activity related to enhanced memory for pleasant and aversive stimuli. *Nature Neuroscience, 2,* 289–293.

Harvey, Gerry. (n.d.). Retrieved December 7, 2006, from http://www.woopidoo .com/business_quotes/authors/gerry-harvey/index.htm

Hattie, J., Biggs, J., & Purdie, N. (1996). Effects of learning skills interventions on student learning: A meta-analysis. *Review of Educational Research, 66*(2), 99–136.

Henry, D. (1994). *Whole language students with low self-direction: A self-assessment tool. Test questionnaire.* (ERIC Document Reproduction Service No. 372359).

Hewlett, W. (2007). *Enhancing your presentation skills.* Retrieved December 29, 2006, from http://www.publicspeakingskills.com/pages/courses/enhancing-your-presentation-skills.htm

Horn, L. (2006). *Placing college graduation rates in context: How 4-year college graduation rates vary with selectivity and the size of low-income enrollment* (NCES 2007–161). Washington, DC: U.S. Department of Education, National Center for Education Statistics.

Huang, Z. (1992). A meta-analysis of student self-questioning strategies. *Dissertation Abstracts International, 52*(11), 38–74.

Institute for Higher Education Policy. (1998). *Reaping the benefits: Defining the public and private value of going to college. The new millennium project on higher education costs, pricing, and productivity.* Washington, DC: Author (ERIC Document Reproduction Service No. 420256).

Jagacinski, C. M., & Nicholls, J. G. (1984). Conceptions of ability and related effects in task involvement and ego involvement. *Journal of Educational Psychology, 76*(5), 909–919.

Jagacinski, C. M., & Nicholls, J. G. (1987). Competence and affect in task involvement and ego involvement: The impact of social comparison information. *Journal of Educational Psychology, 79*(2), 107–114.

James, W. (2000). *Talks to teachers on psychology and to students on some of life's ideals.* New York: Adamant Media.

Jonassen, D. H. (1996). *Computers in the classroom: Mindtools for critical thinking.* Columbus, OH: Charles Merrill.

Jonassen, D., & Marra, R. M. (1994). Concept mapping and other formalisms as mind tools for representing knowledge. *Association of Learning Technology Journal, 2,* 50–56.

Katzenbach, J. R., & Smith, D., K. (1993). The discipline of teams. *Harvard Business Review, 71*(2), 111–120.

Kohn, A. (1986). *The case against competition.* New York: Houghton Mifflin.

Kohn, A. (1993). *Punished by rewards: The trouble with gold stars, incentive plans, A's, praise, and other bribes.* New York: Houghton Mifflin.

Lakein, A. (1974). *How to get control of your time and your life.* New York: Signet.

Lanzing, J. (1997). Students' concept mapping for hypermedia design: Navigation through the world wide web (WWW) space and self-assessment. *Journal of Interactive Learning Research, 8*(3–4), 421–455.

Leamnson, R. (1999). *Thinking about teaching and learning: Developing habits of learning with first year college and university students.* Sterling, VA: Stylus.

Levine, A., & Cureton, J. S. (1998). *When hope and fear collide: A portrait of today's college student* (1st ed.). San Francisco: Jossey-Bass.

Linn, R. E., Baker, E. L., & Dunbar, S. B. (1991). Complex, performance-based assessment: Expectations and validation criteria. *Educational Researcher, 20*(8), 15–21.

Lionni, L. (1970). *Fish is fish.* New York: Scholastic.

Maehr, M. L., & Stallings, R. (1972). Freedom from external evaluation. *Child Development, 43,* 177–185.

Marois, R. (2005). Capacity limits of information processing in the brain. *Trends in Cognitive Sciences, 9*(6), 296–305.

Maslow, A. (2004). *Psychology of science: A reconnaissance.* New York: John Wiley, p. 15.

McCombs, B. (1991). *Meta-cognition and motivation in higher level thinking.* Paper presented at the annual meeting of the American Educational Research Association, Chicago, IL.

McCombs, B. L. (1994). *Development and validation of the learner-centered psychological principles.* Aurora, CO: Mid-continent Regional Educational Laboratory.

McCombs. B. L. (1996). Alternative perspectives for motivation. In L. Baker, P. Afflerbach, & D. Reinking (Eds.), *Developing engaged readers in school and home communities* (pp. 67–87). Hillsdale, NJ: Erlbaum.

Mestre, P. J. (2001). Implications of research on learning for the education of prospective science and physics teachers. *Physics Education, 36,* 44–51.

Middendorf, J., & Kalish, A. (1996). *Frequently asked questions about discussion.* Retrieved December 5, 2006, from http://www.ntlf.com/html/lib/bib/faqdisc.htm

Mitru, G., Millrood, D., & Mateika, J. H. (2002). The impact of sleep on learning and behavior in adolescents. *Teachers College Record, 104*(4), 704–726.

Mueller, J. (2006). *What is authentic assessment?* Retrieved July 24, 2006, from http://jonathan.mueller.faculty.noctrl.edu/toolbox/whatisit.htm

National Research Council. (1996). *National science education standards.* Washington, DC: National Academy Press.

National Research Council. (2000). *How people learn: Brain, mind, experience, and school* (expanded ed.). Washington, DC: National Academy Press.

National Training Laboratories. (1960). *Average retention rate after 24 hours.* Alexandria, VA: Author (originally in Bethel, ME).

Northeastern University. (2006). *Surviving the group project: A note on working in teams.* Retrieved August 1, 2006, from http://web.cba.neu.edu/~ewertheim/teams/ovrvw2.htm

Novak, J. D., & Cañas, A. J. (2006). *The theory underlying concept maps and how to construct them.* Technical Report IHMC Cmap Tools 2006–01. Pensacola, FL: Florida Institute for Human and Machine Cognition.

Novak, J. D., Gowin, D. B., & Johansen, G. T. (1983). The use of concept mapping and knowledge vee mapping with junior high school science students. *Scientific Education, 67*(5), 625–645.

Nystrand, M., & Gamoran, A. (1991a). Instructional discourse, student engagement and literature achievement. *Research in the Teaching of English, 25,* 261–290.

Nystrand, M., & Gamoran, A. (1991b). Student engagement: When recitation becomes conversation. In H. C. Waxman & H. Walberg (Eds.), *Effective teaching: Current research* (pp. 257–276). Berkeley, CA: McCutchan.

Office of Research Education. (1993). *Consumer guide,* Number 2. Washington, DC: U.S. Department of Education.

Ory, J. C., & Ryan, K. (2001). How do student ratings measure up to a new validity framework? In M. Theall, P. Abrami, & L. Mets (eds.), *The student ratings debate: Are they valid? How can we best use them?* New Directions for Institutional Research, no. 109. San Francisco: Jossey-Bass.

Palmer, P. J. (1990). Community, conflict and ways of knowing: Ways to deepen our educational agenda. In J. C. Kendall (Ed.), *Combining service and learning: A resource book for community and public service* (pp. 105–113). Raleigh, NC: National Society for Internships and Experiential Education.

Pintrich, P. R., & Schunk, D. H. (1996). *Motivation in education: Theory, research, and applications.* Columbus, OH: Merrill.

Plotnick, E. (1996). *Trends in educational technology.* Syracuse, NY: ERIC Clearinghouse on Information and Technology (ERIC Document Reproduction Service No. 398861).

Porter, K. (2002). *The value of a college degree* (ERIC Document Reproduction Service No. 470038).

Prince George's County Public Schools. (2006). *A process for designing performance assessment tasks.* Retrieved July 12, 2006, from http://www.pgcps.org/~elc/designsteps1.html

Ramaprasad, A. (1983). On the definition of feedback. *Behavioral Science, 28*(1), 4–13.

Ratey, J. (2002). *A user's guide to the brain: Perception, attention, and the four theaters of the brain* (1st ed.). New York: Vintage Books.

Ridley, D., Schultz, P., Glanz, R., & Weinstein, C. (1992). Self-regulated learning: The interactive influence of meta-cognitive awareness and goal-setting. *Journal of Experimental Education, 60*(4), 293–306.

Roediger, H. Memory: *Explicit and implicit* (Paper presented at the Symposium, Recent Advances in Research on Human Memory). Washington DC: National Academy of Sciences.

Rolheiser, C., & Ross, J. A. (1999). Student self-evaluation—what do we know? *Orbit, 30*(4), 33–36.

Rowe, M. B. (1974). Wait time and rewards as instructional variables: Their influence on language, logic, and fate control: Part II, rewards. *Journal of Research in Science Teaching, 11*(4), 291–308.

Rowley, L. L., & Hurtado, S. (Eds.). (2002). *The non-monetary benefits of an undergraduate education.* Ann Arbor: University of Michigan, Center for the Study of Higher and Postsecondary Education.

Rudner, L. M., & Boston, C. (1994). Performance assessment. *ERIC Review, 3*(1), 2–12.

Sabers, D., Cushing, K. S., & Berliner, D. C. (1991). Differences among teachers in a task characterized by simultaneity, multidimensionality and immediacy. *American Educational Research Journal, 28*(1), 63–88.

Sadler, R. (1989). Formative assessment and the design of instructional systems. *Instructional Science, 18*, 119–144.

Schacter, D. L. (1996). *Searching for memory: The brain, the mind and the past.* New York: Basic Books.

Schacter, D. L. (2001). *The seven sins of memory: How the mind forgets and remembers.* New York: Houghton Mifflin.

Schenck, J. (2003). *Learning, teaching and the brain: Powerful vehicles for enhancing memory (or likewise instruction that works).* ASCD Yearbook, www.ascd.org/portal/sit

Schmolesky, M. T.,Wang, Y., Hanes, D. P., Thompson, K. G., Leutgeb, S., Schall, J. D., et al. (1998). Signal timing across the macaque visual system. *Journal of Neurophysiology, 79*, 3272–3278.

Shaffer, L. S. (1997). A human capital approach to academic advising. *National Academic Advising Association Journal, 17*, 5–12.

Short, D., & Fitzsimmons, S. (2007). *Double the work: Challenges and solutions to acquiring language and academic literacy for adolescent language learners—A report to Carnegie Corporation of New York.* Washington, DC: Alliance for Excellent Education.

Siemens. G. (2004, December 12). *Connectivism: A learning theory for the digital age.* Retrieved from http://www.elearnspace.org/Articles/connectivism.htm

Simon, H. A. (1996). *Observations on the sciences of science learning.* Oral presentation at meeting of the Committee on Developments in the Science of Learning for the Sciences of Science Learning: An Interdisciplinary Discussion, Department of Psychology, Carnegie Mellon University, Washington, DC.

Simon, R. (1980). *Incompatibilität und replikation des resistcnz-plasmids RP4.* Unpublished doctoral dissertation, University or Erlangen, FRG.

Smith, P. (2004). *The quiet crisis: How higher education is failing America.* Bolton, MA: Anker.

Sousa, D. A. (2001). *How the brain learns* (2nd ed.). Thousand Oaks, CA: Corwin Press.

Sprenger, M. (1999). *Learning and memory: The brain in action.* Alexandria, VA: Association for Supervision and Curriculum Development.

Sprenger, M. (2005). Inside Amy's brain. *Educational Leadership, 62*, 28–32.

Springer, L., Stanne, M. E., & Donovan, S. S. (1997). Effects of small-group learning on undergraduates in science, mathematics, engineering and technology: A meta-analysis. *Review of Educational Research, 69*(1), 21–51.

Stahl, R. J. (1994). *Using "think time" and "wait time" skillfully in the classroom* (ERIC Document Reproduction Service No. 370885).

Steinberg, L. (1997). *Beyond the classroom: Why school reform has failed and what parents need to do.* New York: Simon & Schuster.

Stickgold, R. (2000). Inclusive versus exclusive approaches to sleep and dream research. *Behavioral and Brain Science, 23*, 1011–1013.

Stiggins, R. J. (1991). Relevant classroom assessment training for teachers. *Educational Measurement: Issues and Practice, 10*(1), 7–12.

Stix, A. (1997). *Empowering students through negotiable contracting*. Paper presented at the National Middle School Conference, Long Island, New York. (ERIC Document Reproduction Service No. 411274).

Sylwester, R. (1995). *A celebration of neurons: An educator's guide to the human brain*. Alexandria, VA: Association for Supervision and Curriculum Development.

Sylwester, R. (2003). *A biological brain in a cultural classroom: Enhancing cognitive and social development through collaborative classroom management*. Thousand Oaks, CA: Corwin Press.

Tagg, J. (2003). *The learning paradigm college*. Bolton, MA: Anker.

Taylor, R. (2002). *Motivation and learning*. Presented at the National School Conference Institute Conference, Phoenix, AZ.

Terenzini, P. T., Cabrera, A. F., Colbeck, C. L., Parente, J. M., & Bjorklund, S. A. (2001). Collaborative learning vs. lecture/discussion: Students' reported learning gains. *Journal of Engineering Education, 90,* 123–130.

Toffler, A. (1970). *Future shock*. New York: Bantam Books.

University of North Carolina Center for Teaching and Learning. (1991). *Classroom communication analysis project*. Unpublished manuscript.

University of Surrey. (2006). University skills program. Retrieved November 17, 2006, from http://www.surrey.ac.uk/Skills/pack/pedr.html

U.S. Department of Education, National Center for Education Statistics. (1988). *National educational longitudinal study 1988* (NELS 88). Washington, DC: Author.

U.S. Department of Education. (1999). *College for all? Is there too much emphasis on getting a 4-year college degree?* Washington, DC: Author.

U.S. Department of Education. (2000). *National report card on higher education* (No. 10). Washington, DC: Author.

U.S. Department of Education. (2001). *National commission on the high school senior year*. Retrieved May 3, 2006, from http://www.ecs.org/html/Document.asp?chouseid=2929

U.S. Department of Labor, Bureau of Labor Statistics. (2006). *Number of jobs held, labor market activity, and earning growth among the youngest baby boomers: Results from a longitudinal survey*. Retrieved October 4, 2006, from http://www.bls.gov/nls/nlsfaqs.htm#anch41

Vockell, E. L. (2004). *Educational psychology—A practical guide*. Purdue, IN: Purdue University. Retrieved September 17, 2006, from http://www.education.calumet.purdue.edu/vockell/EdPsyBook

Voss, J. F., Greene, T. R., Post, T. A., & Penner, B. C. (1983). Problem solving skills in the social sciences. In G. H. Bower (Ed.), *The psychology of learning and motivation: Advances in research and theory* (vol. 17, pp. 165–213). New York: Academic Press.

Vygotsky, L. S. (1978). *Mind in society: The development of higher psychological processes*. Cambridge, MA: Harvard University Press.

Weimer, M. (2002). *Learner-centered teaching: Five key changes to practice* (1st ed.). San Francisco: Jossey-Bass.

White, B. Y., & Frederiksen, J. R. (1998). Inquiry, modeling, and metacognition: Making science accessible to all students. *Cognition and Instruction, 16*(1), 3–118.

Whitford, P. (1995). The five most important life-long job search skills. Modern Job Search Concepts. *ENET Educational Society Newsletter*.

Wiggins, G. (1990). The case for authentic assessment. *Practical Assessment, Research & Evaluation, 2*(2). Retrieved November 4, 2006, from http://PAREon line.net/getvn.asp?v = 2&n = 2

Willimon, W. H., & Naylor, T. H. (1995). *The abandoned generation: Rethinking higher education*. Grand Rapids, MI: Eerdmans.

Winn, W., & Snyder, D. (1996). Cognitive perspectives in psychology. In D. H. Jonassen (Ed.), *Handbook of research for educational communications and technology* (pp. 112–142). New York: Simon & Schuster.

Woods, D. R. (1994). *Problem-based learning: How to gain the most from PBL*. Watertown, Ontario: Donald R. Woods.

Wright, P., & Lickorish, A. (1983). Proof-reading texts on screen and paper. *Behavior and Information Technology, 2*(3), 227–235.

Zull, J. (2002). *The art of changing the brain: Enriching the practice of teaching by exploring the biology of learning* (1st ed.). Sterling, VA: Stylus.

INDEX

Italics indicate figures or tables